The Concept of Sentence and Meaning

The Concept of Sentence and Meaning

Vistas in Indian Milieu

Sarath P. Nath

With a Foreword by
P. Narayanan Namboodiri

DK PRINTWORLD
Publishers of Indian Traditions

Cataloging in Publication Data — DK
[Courtesy: D.K. Agencies (P) Ltd. <docinfo@dkagencies.com>]

Nath, Sarath P., 1987- author.
The concept of sentence and meaning : vistas in Indian milieu / Sarath P. Nath; with a foreword by P. Narayanan Namboodiri.
pages cm
Includes text in Sanskrit (roman).
Includes bibliographical references.
ISBN 9788124610671 (hardbound)

1. Bhartṛhari. Vākyapadīya. 2. Sanskrit language – Sentences. 3. Sanskrit language – Philosophy. I. Title.

LCC PK811.N38 2023 | DDC 491.25 23

ISBN 978-81-246-1067-1 (Hardbound)
First published in India in 2023

Printed and published by:
D.K. Printworld (P) Ltd.
Regd. Office: "Vedaśrī", F-395, Sudarshan Park
ESI Hospital Metro Station, New Delhi - 110015
Phones: (011) 2545-3975; 2546-6019
e-mail: indology@dkprintworld.com
Website: www.dkprintworld.com

Foreword

MEANING of the word "meaning" was a great concern for the Indian thinkers. In order to finalize this, they have examined and taken into consideration all the components of a communicative unit such as syllables, words, sentences and intentions of the speakers as well as the capacity to group. After this examination, different philosophers – Mīmāṁsakas, Naiyāyikas and Śābdikas – have arrived the conclusion that sentence is the essential component to convey a sense of meaning to a listener. The theory of *akhaṇḍa-vākya* is based on the indivisible *sphoṭa* theory and the sentence-meaning is experienced by the concept of *pratibhā*. The division of sentence as per the priority of words occurred on the basis of mutual expectancy by which the intended meaning may be assumed by the listener.

Mīmāṁsakas consider *bhāvanā* (action) which is the most essential segment to understand the sense of uttered syllables. On the one hand, the Naiyāyikas emphasize the priority of the words ending in Nominative case. The grammarians, on the other hand, stress the need of predominance to *vyāpāra* for attaining the meaning. Thus various philosophers have put forward different concepts of sentence, which are the basis of various linguistic aspects.

The *Vākyapadīya* of Bhartṛhari (sixth century CE) is a text which elaborately explains the notions on sentence. Philosophical dimensions of grammatical units are systematically presented here. The author of this book Dr Sarath P. Nath has attempted to present the philosophy of language in a Bhartṛharian perspective. To substantiate his views, syntactic and semantic thoughts in India are elaborately discussed. While explaining the philosophy, a detailed study on Bhartṛhari is also conducted here.

Various perspectives on the concept of sentence in Indian system of knowledge are taken to consider in the second chapter by which, the limitations of their arguments can be critically evaluated in the following chapter.

Eightfold theory of the sentence propounded by Bhartṛhari is vividly examined here. The illustrations given to each definition by the commentators of Bhartṛhari are described here properly. The views of our ancestors are also critically promoted.

The concept of *pratibhā* is a topic of discussion in Indian intellectual domain. Rhetoricians, philosophers, critics and commentators have viewed this phenomenon from various angles. The author also attempts to justify the concept of *pratibhā* explained by Bhartṛhari in accordance with the views already prevailed in this circle.

I am extremely happy to congratulate Dr Sarath P. Nath for bringing out a composition on the philosophy of Bhartṛhari on sentence. Though the significance of the work can only be understood by those scholars who are well studied in Helārāja and Puṇyarāja, it will remain an asset to the field of grammatical deliberations.

Professor Dr P. Narayanan Namboodiri
Professor of Sanskrit (retd)
Department of Sanskrit
University of Calicut

Preface

LANGUAGE is generally perceived as the method of communication. It is essentially a social phenomenon through which we share our thoughts, experiences, emotions, commands, wishes, statements of facts, etc. Thus, the basic function of language is "communication". Ancient Indian scholars inquired into this concept and went beyond its mere communicative perspective. They portrayed it as the lamp that brought to light all the material objects. Had there been no language, everything would have remained in the darkness of ignorance. No knowledge or science would have originated. Nobody can fulfil his/her life in this material world, without the medium of language. Language which thus spreads over all walks of life is not just a medium of communication, based on syllable–word–sentence. Language can be perceived as the carrier of thoughts and ideas. Thus, beyond its communicative level, language is something, which carries within itself the entire culture of a community. Therefore, an insight into the working of language can be the beginning of the philosophical inquiry.

One of the fundamental problems in the philosophy of language, that has attracted the serious attention of all thinkers, is the relation between *śabda* (linguistic element) and its *artha* (meaning). The term *śabda* is normally used to refer to a linguistic element, which is the meaningful unit of speech. Indian thinkers uphold different views on the linguistic element that is referred to by the term *śabda*. According to various thinkers, it is the articulated phoneme (*varṇa*) or the word (*pada*) or the sentence (*vākya*). But all of them emphasize the role of sentence in communicating the ideas conceived by the speaker. Therefore the study of sentence and sentence-meaning became one of the major concerns of linguists, grammarians and philosophers.

The present book puts stress upon the different prospects regarding the basic element of the language-sentence and its meaning. The studies on sentence and sentence-meaning in ancient India are disseminated among the different systems of knowledge. The scholars in the schools of Mīmāṁsā, Nyāya and Vyākaraṇa have devoted their effort to unravel the basic problems regarding these concepts. While analysing the concept of sentence, ancient thinkers tried to deal with two vexed questions: What is a sentence? and What constitutes the sentence-meaning? They have endeavoured to answer these questions according to their preconceived notions.

In the science of Grammar, it was Bhartṛhari, the great grammarian and philosopher, who discovered the depth and breadth of Sanskrit grammar. His magnum opus the *Vākyapadīya* created a philosophical dimension in the science of Grammar hitherto unseen. He explains the concept of language in different levels to have a comprehensive idea of its function. If language is perceived in the communicative level, sentence is the basic unit of language. The entire second *kāṇḍa* of *Vākyapadīya* is dedicated for the syntactico–semantic analysis of the sentence. Here, Bhartṛhari sets forth new visions and dimensions in the concept of sentence and sentence-meaning. His whole theory of language is to be understood from the context of his general theory of *akhaṇḍa-vākya*. According to this theory, a sentence is the indivisible *sphoṭa* or a unitary whole and the sentence-meaning is the kind of a flash of understanding called *pratibhā*. The present study tries to analyse the concepts and discussions on sentence and sentence-meaning, with special stress to the *Vākyapadīya*.

Today, language study possesses a multidimensional perspective, which has moved up even into the realm of the studies on history, culture, psychology and philosophy. In this scenario, an inquiry into the linguistic perspectives of ancient Indian thinkers is useful and appropriate. The present study tries to understand the sentence theory of Bhartṛhari in a deeper level and find out whether his unnoticed ideas could be useful in interpreting the language phenomenon. Bhartṛhari's concepts are studied by many scholars of the East and West. Though many of his concepts are treated as mystic entities, the linguistic value of his views on sentence and sentence-meaning is unravelled by modern scholars. But the ideas of *akhaṇḍa-vākyasphoṭa*, *pratibhā*, etc. are either taken for granted or are not given much importance in the linguistic point of view. Therefore it is significant to analyse these concepts wherever available rather than keeping them away because of their philosophical or metaphysical label on them.

The book comprises of four chapters. The first chapter entitled "The Philosophy of Language: A Bhartṛharian Perspective" discusses the syntactic and semantic thoughts in India and the importance of Bhartṛhari in Indian linguistic tradition. A brief survey of Bhartṛhari's works and the commentaries of *Vākyapadiya* is also included in this chapter.

The second chapter elaborately discusses various definitions of sentence propounded by different schools of thought. The different views of ancient Sanskrit scholars on the relation among the words in a sentence and their meanings, through which they are semantically connected to give a unified sense, are also explained in detail.

The third chapter includes the discussion of the concepts of Bhartṛhari on sentence and sentence-meaning. It begins with presenting the definitions of sentence which are enumerated in the first verses of the second *kāṇḍa* of *Vākyapadīya*. In the second part, different ideas on the concept of sentence-meaning discussed by Bhartṛhari are analysed and Bhartṛhari's concept of *pratibhā* as the meaning of sentence is also pointed out.

The fourth chapter discusses the origin and development of the concept of *pratibhā* in various systems of knowledge. The characteristics of Bhartṛhari's *pratibhā* and the implications of this very concept are also explained in this chapter. The book concludes with the conspectus of the important points noted during the study. The scope for the further study in the topic is also pointed out.

At this juncture, I thankfully remember my supervising teacher Professor P. Narayanan Namboodiri, who was kind enough to write a Foreword to this book and his proper guidance and wholehearted support that helped me to materialize this work. I am grateful to Professor C. Rajendran, whose valuable suggestions helped me in choosing the topic of the study. I am deeply obliged to my teachers Professor R. Vasudevan Potti, Professor O. Vatsala and Professor Krishnakumar, whose blessings made me confident to endure in Sanskrit grammar. I am particularly thankful to Dr Ajithan P.I., whose timely interventions and continuous support helped me a lot.

It would be really unkind if I do not thank my wife who stood as a pillar for me to lean on during the difficult phases of my research. Also, I thank all my family members, teachers and friends who supported me in different ways during my research.

Dr Sarath P. Nath

Contents

1

The Philosophy of Language

A Bhartṛharian Perspective

The Concept of Language: Indian Perspectives

LANGUAGE can be defined as the method of human communication, either spoken or written, consisting of the use of words in a structural and conventional way (https://en.oxforddictionaries.com/definition/language). The word "language" has its origin from the Old French word *langage* and from the Latin word *lingua*. The word *lingua* in Latin signifies "tongue". Thus the word "language" simply denotes the human interaction, which involves gestures and spoken or written words. A human being thinks and, as a necessary corollary of his thinking, he wishes to communicate the ideas conceived. Language, as a tool of communication, achieves its goal, when the listener understands what the speaker intends to convey. Thus, thought and language are the two characteristics that differentiate man from animals. Aldous Huxley states that "for in spite of language, in spite of intelligence and intuition and sympathy, one can never really communicate anything to anybody" (2000: 3). Harold Coward rightly observes that "language is a fascinating aspect of human behaviour and it not only makes distinction between man and animals, but mediates human knowledge also" (1980: 1). Thus, language can rather be perceived as the very essence of thought, than a mere tool of communication.

Language has been one of the fundamental concerns of Indian schools of thought and has attracted the serious attention of all thinkers from the outset. They perceived language as one of the most precious gifts given by God to human beings (*samskr̥tam nāma daivī vāganvākhyātā maharṣibhiḥ* – *Kāvyādarśa* 1.33). All knowledge from the time immemorial had been handed over to us in the form of language. Bhartr̥hari also mentions that there is no cognition without the operation of the word and all knowledge is illuminated by language:

> *na so 'sti pratyayo loke yaḥ śabdānugamādr̥te* ।
> *anuviddhamiva jñānam sarvam śabdena bhāsate* ॥
> – *Vākyapadīya* I.123

Thus, it can be stated that the ancient preceptors were aware of the importance of language in our social life. In the study of language, they tried to deal with various vexed questions like: What is language? What is its structure? How can it be analysed? They have been endeavoured to solve these problems according to the basic norms of their philosophies.

The Philosophy of Language

In India, the study of language has never been the monopoly of the grammarians or the rhetoricians. Almost all schools of thoughts have given emphasis to the fundamental problems of verbal communication. The earlier references of linguistic thoughts in India are glimpsed in the Vedas and Upaniṣads. The Vedic seers praised language as a powerful deity, known as Vāk, who bestows all the favours to its devotees. In the *R̥gveda*, a complete *sūkta* in the glorification of Vāk can be found. Even more examples can be cited from the *R̥gveda* which show the prominence of Vāk. It states that those who do not understand the real nature of Vāk cannot see language, even when they are seeing and cannot hear it, even when they are hearing. The Vāk unfolds herself only to those, who understand the essence of speech.

> *uta tvaḥ paśyanna dadarśa vācamuta tvaḥ śṛṇvanna śṛṇotyenām* ।
> *uto tvasmai tanvaṁ vi sasre jāyeva patya uśatī suvāsāḥ* ॥
> – *ṚV* X.71.4

The seers of *Ṛgveda* praise the speech as the great deity (Mahādeva), who possesses himself in humans.

> *catvāri śṛṅgā trayo asya pādā dve śīrṣe sapta hastāso asya* ।
> *tridhā baddho vṛṣabho roravīti maho devo martyāṁ ā viveśa* ॥
> –IV.58.3

Apart from the Vedic passages, three among the six Vedāṅgas are directly concerned with language, viz. Vyākaraṇa (Grammar), Nirukta (Etymology) and Śikṣā (Phonetics). This indicates the prominence of linguistic study in the Vedic age.

The study of linguistic aspects has been emphasized in all systems of Indian philosophy. The schools of Mīmāṁsā and Vyākaraṇa have contributed much in this regard. Pūrva-Mīmāṁsā is also known as Vākyaśāstra, which is devoted in interpreting sentences, either Vedic or ordinary. The Nyāya system, known as Pramāṇaśāstra, also discusses the basic linguistic problems. Though the school of Vyākaraṇa does not possess the status of *darśana* (philosophy), the ancient grammarians were interested in the linguistic and philosphical analysis of speech and they claimed the status of an independent *darśana*.

The Basic Problems of the Philosophy of Language

The Indian approach to the study of language has been characterized by both analysis and synthesis. The study of language essentially requires a process of analysis in which the speech utterance is analysed in terms of sentences and words, stems and suffixes, morphemes and phonemes.[1] The earlier reference regarding the language analysis can be seen in the *Taittirīya Saṁhitā*. It says that once gods (*devas*) requested Lord Indra to analyse speech and on behalf of their request, he performed the duty. Since then, the speech is called *vaikr̥ta* (analysed) (VI.4.7). Śākalya's *Padapāṭha* of *R̥gveda* is also one of the earlier attempts of language analysis. The *R̥gveda*, originally in the *saṁhitā* form, has been broken down into words in this *Padapāṭha*. In the *Br̥haddevatā*, Śaunaka defines a sentence as the group of words and words as the group of phonemes (2.117). We can find similar analytical methodology in Prātiśākhyas also. But the systematic analysis of speech begins from the time of Yāska, who analysed the speech on the basis of etymology. He was the first to divide language into four parts; *nāma* (noun), *ākhyāta* (verb), *upasarga* (prefixes) and *nipāta* (prepositions) (*tat yānyetāni catvāri padajātāni nāmākhyāte copasarganipātāśca* – *Nirukta*, 2002: 3). This fourfold analysis is accepted by almost all the later Indian systems of knowledge.

The whole system of Vyākaraṇa has been dedicated in the linguistic analysis of speech. Pāṇini, who propounded the descriptive grammar of Sanskrit language in his *Aṣṭādhyāyī*, has been praised by many modern linguists. The *Aṣṭādhyāyī* is primarily concerned with building up of words from verbal roots, preverbs, primary and secondary suffixes, and nominal and verbal terminations. This treatise also points out some syntactic problems involved in the formation of compound words and the relationship of the nouns in a sentence with the verb. The followers of the Pāṇinian school developed this analytical method of language study in their works.

---

1 This analytical method is very popular in Sanskrit. Generally this method is considered as older, but some scholars like Punita Sharma holds that it is a later development in the history of language (1998: 12).

The school of Mīmāṁsā is mainly concerned with the methodology of textual interpretation of the Vedic texts. Mīmāṁsakas use both analysis and synthesis in their approach to the problems of textual interpretation. They give the semantic definition of the sentence and introduce the concepts of *ākāṅkṣā* (mutual expectancy), *yogyatā* (consistency) and *āsatti* (congruity), which are necessary for the unity of the sentence. Naiyāyikas hold that *śabda*, uttered by a trustworthy person, is one of the means of valid knowledge. Therefore, the method of language analysis has been occupied a prime position in their philosophy. Thus, it is clear that the various schools in India have carried out significant studies, which have produced insights into the working of language (Coward and Raja 2008: 5).

Syntactic and Semantic Thoughts in India

One of the fundamental aspects of the philosophy of language, that has attracted the serious attention of all thinkers, is the relation between *śabda* (the linguistic element) and its meaning (*artha*). The term *śabda* is normally used to refer to a linguistic element, which is the meaningful unit of speech. Philosophers held different views on the linguistic element that is referred to by the term *śabda*. According to various systems, it is the articulated sound or the phoneme (*varṇa*) or the word (*pada*) or the sentence (*vākya*). Mīmāṁsakas consider the letters or phonemes as *śabda*, which is eternal. Words and sentences are only the manifestations of these phonemes. For the Naiyāyikas, the term *śabda* refers to the word which is produced by the speaker and heard by the listener. Therefore, *śabda* is impermanent for them. According to the *sphoṭa* theory of grammarians, *śabda* is eternal, but not in the form of letters. To Bhartṛhari, *śabda* is the complete utterance of the sentence and is the unit of language called *vākya-sphoṭa* (ibid.). Grammarians analyse the sentence also into morphemes for grammatical purpose, which are termed as *pada-sphoṭa* and *varṇa-sphoṭa*.

The Concept of Sentence

As discussed, language is perceived as the method of communicating one's thoughts. An idea or a thought can never be in bits and pieces, but is a unitary whole. Thus, it is communicated also as a unitary whole, but not in terms of its parts. Since words cannot communicate the speaker's thought fully, sentence is to be considered as the unit of language, which can communicate the whole idea. Different thinkers accept either a letter or a word or a sentence as the unit of language. But all of them emphasize the role of sentence in communicating the ideas conceived by the speaker. Therefore, the study of sentence and sentence-meaning became the most important concept for linguists, grammarians and philosophers. Though we cannot find any explicit discussions on this topic in the ancient literature, some glimpses can be seen in Vedic texts. As stated, a simple definition of sentence is cited in the *Bṛhaddevatā*. Later, Naiyāyikas and Mīmāṁsakas have expounded the syntactico–semantic analysis of sentence. They have produced several independent treatises on the systematic analysis of sentence. In Sanskrit grammar, the emphasis has been given to *prakriyā* (formative aspect of words), while the treatises on the syntactico–semantic analysis of sentence are a few and far between. The *Vākyapadīya* of Bhartṛhari, *Vaiyākaraṇabhūṣaṇasāra* of Kauṇḍabhaṭṭa, *Paramalaghumañjūṣā* of Nāgeśa, etc. have completely devoted their attention to this topic. Among them, the *Vākyapadīya* possesses a prime position in the realm of the philosophy of language.

Bhartṛhari: The Philosopher Linguist

Bhartṛhari is considered as an outstanding figure in the history of Indian linguistic thought. He led grammar into philosophy proper, by making a case for Vyākaraṇa as a *darśana*, a view about ultimate things, eventually about liberation. Gaurinath Sastri therefore aptly refers to his work as an "astoundingly original system of thought which to the best of my knowledge has no parallel" (1959: xxiv). The *Vākyapadīya* became the most extensive work in the medieval period which represented the most fruitful epoch of Indian thought. Bhartṛhari was also the major architect of *sphoṭa* theory, which is regularly identified as the contribution of grammarians to the philosophical problem of meaning. His linguistic philosophy is to be considered as unique and singular among the linguistic thoughts in India.

DATE OF BHARTṚHARI

Although Bhartṛhari is a renowned grammarian, philosopher and author in Sanskrit literature, we have very little information about his personal life and date. There are references of many Bhartṛharis and one may find different traditions about him in different places. Bhaṭṭi, the author of the grammatical poem *Bhaṭṭikāvya*, was also known as Bhartṛhari. There are references to another Bhartṛhari, who was the ruler of Mālwā, in Tāranātha's *History of Buddhism* (Tāranātha 1990). He also mentions a Bhartṛhari who was intimately connected to the king and one of the nine great *siddhas* of the Nāthapanthīya religious order. But neither the king nor the *siddha* is known to have been a poet (Sarma 1969: 8). One of the traditions says that Bhartṛhari was the youngest son of a brāhmaṇa who had four wives from four different castes and that Bhartṛhari was the son of his śūdra wife. Another tradition says that Bhartṛhari was a king, perhaps a brother of either Vikramāditya or Śūdraka, who gave up his worldly life and became a *saṁnyāsin*. Bhartṛhari's life has been dramatized by Harihara in his *Bhartṛharinirveda*. In this story, Bhartṛhari is portrayed as a student of Gorakṣanātha, from whom he learnt Yoga and renounced the world (Coward 1980: 11).

However, these traditions cannot be taken as evidence to fix the date of Bhartṛhari. Since he had commented upon the *Mahābhāṣya* of Patañjali (150 BCE), the date of *Mahābhāṣya* can be taken as the upper limit. His major work the *Vākyapadīya* is referred to by Vāmana and Jayāditya in *Kāśikāvṛtti* (650 CE).

> *adhikṛtya kṛte granthe* । – *MB* 4.3.87
>
> *śiśukrandayamasabhadvandvendra-jananādibhiśchaḥ* ।
> – *MB* 4.3.88
>
> *taditi vartate* । *adhikṛtya kṛte granthe iti ca* । *dvandvāt (dvitīyāsamarthāt) chaḥ pratyayo bhavati adhikṛtya kṛte granthe* । *śabdārtasambandhīyam prakaraṇam* ।
> – *Vākyapadīya* under *MB* 4.3.87-88

Hence Bhartṛhari can be placed within the limits 150 BCE – 650 CE. Much of the evidence regarding his date supports him being placed nearer to the latter date. I-tsing, the Chinese traveller and a Buddhist, who studied at the Nālandā monastery in 670 CE, reported Bhartṛhari died forty years earlier. If this report is accepted as authentic, Bhartṛhari probably died in 630 CE. But I-tsing also reported that Bhartṛhari was a contemporary of Dharmapāla, who lived during 530-61 CE. Here it can be noted that I-tsing's opinions are self-contradictory and unacceptable. More reliable evidence can be seen in the Tibetan translation of *Traikālya Parīkṣā* of the famous Buddhist author Diṅnāga. He quotes two verses from the *Svopajñavṛtti* (hereafter *Vṛtti*) of the *Vākyapadīya*. This evidently says that Bhartṛhari must have preceded Diṅnāga, who flourished between 480 and 540 CE. Some autobiographical references can be seen at the end of the second *kāṇḍa* of *Vākyapadīya*, where he mentions his teacher with great respect (2.478-87). Puṇyarāja, in his commentary, makes it clear that it is Vasurāṭa, the teacher of Bhartṛhari (*Vākyapadīya* 2.481). The Tibetan translations of Diṅnāga and some works of a Jaina writer Siṁhasūrigaṇi suggest that Vasurāṭa was a brāhmaṇa and a brother-in-law of Bālāditya, a pupil of the great Buddhist scholar Vasubandhu, whose date is fixed as 400 CE (Coward 1980: 11).

We can collect many references supporting the latter date limit of Bhartṛhari. In the *Śatapatha Brāhmaṇa*, while commenting on the portion *vāgvā anuṣṭub, vāco vā idam sarvam prabhavati* (1.3.2.16), Hariswāmi quotes two verses from the *Vākyapadīya* as follows:

> *vāco vā ityādi* । *vācaḥ śabdasya sakāśāt 'idam' sarvamarthajātaṁ prabhavati* । *ata eva jagataḥ śabdavivartamāhuḥ* । *tadyathā-anādinidhanaṁ brahma śabdatattvaṁ yadakṣaram vivartate 'rthabhāvena prakriyā jagato yataḥ* । *iti* । *tathānyatrāpi śabdavedhāt tatkāryatvam arthasyoktam-na so 'sti pratyayo loke yaḥ śābdānugamādṛte anuviddhamiva jñānaṁ sarvaṁ śabdena bhāsate* । *iti* ।
>
> – I.3.2.16

Hariswāmi was evidently lived in the sixth century CE. Another important reference that historians point out is that of Kumārila Bhaṭṭa who flourished in the fifth century CE. He quotes several verses of the *Vākyapadīya* in his famous work *Tantravārtika*. In the light of all these discussions, it may be deduced that the date of Bhartṛhari can be fixed between 450 and 500 CE.

WORKS OF BHARTṚHARI

There are several philosophical, grammatical and literary works attributed to Bhartṛhari. Coward mentions five works which are attributed to Bhartṛhari (1976: 12). They are:

1. *Mahābhāṣyaṭīkā*: a commentary named *Dīpikā* on the *Mahābhāṣya* of Patañjali of which, only a fragment still exists.
2. *Vākyapadīya*, chapters I-III: Bhartṛhari's great work on the Sanskrit philosophy of language.

3. *Vṛtti* on *Vākyapadīya* I and II: a commentary explaining the above work.[2]
4. The *Śabdadhātusamīkṣā*: a work that is currently lost.
5. *Śatakas* on the *Nīti*, *Śṛṅgāra* and *Vairāgya*: well-known Sanskrit poems on politics, passionate love and renunciation.

We can undoubtedly fix that Bhartṛhari, the grammarian-philosopher, is the author of *Mahābhāṣyaṭīkā*, viz. *Mahābhāṣyadīpikā*, *Vākyapadīya* and *Vṛtti*, in the light of many evidences. Vardhamāna Sūri, a Jaina grammarian, says about two works of Bhartṛhari in his *Gaṇaratnamahodadhi* as

> *bhartṛhariḥ vākyapadīyaprakīrṇakayoḥ kartā Mahābhāṣya-tripādyāḥ vyākhyātā ca* । – 1963: 2

Another grammatical work of Bhartṛhari, *Śabdadhātusamīkṣā*, has unfortunately not come to light so far. But, there is little evidence to prove that the author of the literary work *Śatakatraya* and the grammarian Bhartṛhari are the same. Sarma, while introducing the text *Puruṣārthopadeśa*, which is also attributed to Bhartṛhari, clearly states that "the grammarian Bhartṛhari mentioned by the Chinese traveller I-tsing is different from the author of *Vākyapadīyam* and *Mahābhāṣyadīpikā*" (1969: 8).

---

[2] Recent studies of scholars like Ashok Aklujkar claim that the *Vṛtti* of the first two cantos of *Vākyapadīya* cannot be attributed to Bhartṛhari. The first two cantos, according to one manuscript tradition, consist of *kārikā*s as well as *Vṛtti*. The other manuscript traditions have only the *kārikā*s, accompanied by a *ṭīkā*, evidently authored by someone other than the *kārikā* author (1972: 181-98).

In the *Vṛtti* of the first canto, the author states that his name is Harivṛṣabha (2008: 236). Many scholars in Sanskrit treat Bhartṛhari and Harivṛṣabha as one, but Aklujkar argues that Harivṛṣabha is different from Bhartṛhari. According to him, Harivṛṣabha (Bhartṛhari) is the author of the commentary *Paddhati* (2008: 179).

MAHĀBHĀṢYADĪPIKĀ

It is evidently known that Bhartṛhari has written a commentary on the *Mahābhāṣya* of Patañjali. Unfortunately only one manuscript of this work is available till now, which has the commentary up to *Mahābhāṣya* 1.1.55. In the colophon of this manuscript, the name of the commentary is given as *Bhartṛhariṭīkā*, *Mahābhāṣyaṭīkā* and *Mahābhāṣyadīpikā* (*Mahābhāṣya*, Preface, 1984: 3). Ashok Aklujkar points out that, "early commentators in the grammatical tradition refer to this work as *Tripādī*, which signifies that the commentary is only up to the third *pāda* of *Aṣṭādhyāyī*" (2008: 122). Kaiyaṭa, in the beginning of his commentary *Pradīpa* on the *Mahābhāṣya* refers to *Dīpikā* as:

> *bhāṣyābdhiḥ kvātigambhīraḥ kvāhaṁ mandamatistathā*
> *chātrāṇāmupahāsyatvaṁ yāsyāmi piśunātmanā* ।
> *tathāpi haribaddhena sāreṇa granthasetunā*
> *kramamāṇaiḥ śanaiḥ pāraṁ tasya prāptāsmi paṅguvat* ॥
> – Introductory verses 6-7

These lines throw light to two facts that Kaiyaṭa must have had before him a complete text of Bhartṛhari's *Mahābhāṣyadīpikā* and the authenticity of the commentary was also unquestionable.

VĀKYAPADĪYA

The *Vākyapadīya* can be treated as the magnum opus of Bhartṛhari. This is probably the first book which laid down a new pathway to the philosophy of grammar in India. Later, philosopher-grammarians like Kauṇḍabhaṭṭa and Nāgeśa accept the *Vākyapadīya* as the authentic text to explain their views. Subramania Iyer opines that "not only grammarians but other Indian philosophers also admitted the authenticity of this work" (2006: 2). The word *Vākyapadīya* is derived from two words, viz. *vākya* (sentence) and *pada* (word). As stated, the derivation of this word is explained by Vāmana and Jayāditya in *Kāśikā* (under *MB* 4.3.87-88). Hence the title *Vākyapadīya* signifies "a work which is related to *vākya* and *pada*". According to this derivation, the text *Vākyapadīya* elaborately discusses the concepts of word and sentence, which are the main topics in it.

STRUCTURAL ANALYSIS OF VĀKYAPADĪYA

The *Vākyapadīya* is consisted of three chapters (*kāṇḍa*s) and because of this reason, it is termed as *trikāṇḍī* by some scholars.[3] The first chapter is called Āgamakāṇḍa or Brahmakāṇḍa. But in the colophon of first chapter, the name of the chapter is given as Āgamasamuccaya or Brahmakāṇḍa:

> *iti śrīmad padavākyapramāṇajñamahopādhyāya bhartṛharikṛte vākyapadīye āgamasamuccayo nāma prathamaṁ brahmakāṇḍam* – 2006: 282

This chapter elucidates the real nature of the speech element *śabda-tattva* or *śabda-brahma* which is eternal and beyond birth and death. The first four verses of the first canto of *Vākyapadīya* give a vivid picture of *śabda-brahma*, which is the sum total of Bhartṛhari's theory of language. He describes *śabda-tattva* as the all-pervaded essence of the universe, from which the whole world is derived. His arguments in the whole *Vākyapadīya* can be traced to this concept of *śabda-tattva*. Probably, Bhartṛhari is the first to proclaim word (*śabda*) as eternal *Brahman* in the history of Indian philosophy.[4]

---

3 Aklujkar holds a different opinion that only the first two *kāṇḍa*s constitute the text *Vākyapadīya*. He argues that the title *Vākyapadīya* could have referred to the second of the three cantos. The third canto named Padakāṇḍa or Prakīrṇakāṇḍa (which means miscellaneous) seems to be no older than sixteenth century CE (Coward and Raja 2008: 547-55).

4 Later, a similar reference can be seen in the *Kāvyādarśa* of Daṇḍin. He states that unless the light called language shines in the world, it would sink in deep darkness:

→

Bhartṛhari says that the one and indivisible *śabda-tattva* apparently seems to be many, due to its different inherent factors[5] (*Vākyapadīya* I.2). Bhartṛhari says that the real nature of *śabda* or *śabda-tattva* is not external, but it is the inner consciousness. Bhartṛhari explains this *śabda-tattva* in two dimensions. He perceives *śabda-tattva* as the essence of language, which is described as *Brahman* and is not external. He also views *śabda-tattva* as the cause of verbal cognition (*sphoṭa*). Hence we can find that Bhartṛhari manifests language in its metaphysical background and as a tool of communication. According to Bhartṛhari, every expression contains three elements: (i) *dhvani* (uttered sound), (ii) *sphoṭa* (the intermediary or the sound image from which bears meaning), and (iii) *artha* (meaning). Bhartṛhari discusses the first two in the first *kāṇḍa* of *Vākyapadīya*. The third element, which is a multidimensional entity, is elaborately discussed in the second canto.

Along with *śabda-tattva*, Bhartṛhari discusses other relevant topics also in this chapter. The importance and advantages of studying grammar, authenticity of Āgamas or Vedas, the real nature of *śabda*, discussions about *sphoṭa* and *dhvani*, *apabhraṁśa,* etc. are the major topics dealt with in this chapter. After describing the characteristics of *śabda-brahma*, Bhartṛhari suggests that the Vedas are the way to manifest this *śabda-tattva*. Here we may find a detailed discussion on the authenticity of the Vedas and other *pramāṇas*. He accepts the Vedas as one, compiled by many sages and therefore it became many (*Vākyapadīya* I.5). Various Darśanas and Śāstras are also derived from the same Veda by various philosophers (*Vākyapadīya* I.7). Grammar should be considered

← *idamandham tamaḥ kṛtsnam jāyeta bhuvanatrayam* ।
yadi śabāhvayam jyotirāsamsāram na dīpyate । – 1.4

5 This concept of *śabda-brahman* seems to be similar with that of "Brāhmāṇa" in Vedānta. But when it is analysed thoroughly, it cannot be analogous with the concept of Brāhmaṇa.

as the main Vedāṅga according to Bhartṛhari, for it is the only way to know the real nature of *śabda* and through which, we can attain the final goal *apavarga* (*taddvāramapavargasya vāṅmalānāṁ cikitsitam* – *Vākyapadīya* I.14).

As indicated, Bhartṛhari defines *śabda* in two dimensions: one is the cause and the other is the external word that we utter. The former is termed as *sphoṭa* and the latter as *dhvani* or *vaikharī*. Patañjali also explains *śabda* in this manner in the first chapter of *Mahābhāṣya:*

> *yenoccāritena sāsnālāṅgūlakakudakhuraviṣāṇinām saṁpratyayo bhavati sa śabdaḥ* । – 1991, vol. I: 11

Bhartṛhari explicates the nature of *sphoṭa* and *dhvani* in this canto. He analyses this concept from the point of view of the speaker as well as the hearer. While we analyse *śabda* in the speaker's dimension, *sphoṭa* is the cause of *vaikharī* (uttered sound). The order is reversed when *śabda* is analysed from the hearer's point of view. What is worthy of note here is in both cases *sphoṭa* is the meaning-bearing unit.

Bhartṛhari sets forth *sphoṭa* as the real *śabda* in the first chapter and a detailed study on the concept of sentence is included in the second chapter, Vākyakāṇḍa. While we enter into this chapter, various views about the definition of sentence can be found. Bhartṛhari elucidates two main views regarding the concept of sentence. According to some philosophers, sentence is indivisible (*akhaṇḍa*) while in some others' view, sentence is an aggregation of its parts and thus, it can be divided into parts or it is *sakhaṇḍa*. Bhartṛhari is in favour of the *akhaṇḍa-pakṣa* (indivisibility of sentence), for he clearly states in the first chapter that words in a sentence and syllables in a word are not true, but only imaginary.

pade na varṇā vidyante varṇeṣvavayavā na ca ।
vākyāt padānām atyantaṁ praviveko na kaścana ॥
– *Vākyapadīya* I.73

Along with these eight views on sentence, Bhartr̥hari discusses the definitions given by Kātyāyana, the author of *vārtika*s and Jaimini, the founder of Mīmāṁsā philosophy. After explaining these views, Bhartr̥hari affirms the indivisibility theory of sentence through the Vākyavādin–Padavādin controversy and refutes the Padavādins, who do not accept the authenticity of sentence.

Various views on sentence-meaning by different thinkers are also discussed in this chapter. Bhartr̥hari elucidates the theories of *anvitābhidhāna* and *abhihitānvaya*, the two prominent theses propounded by Padavādins. He then discusses the *pratibhā* theory of sentence-meaning, in which the meaning of a sentence is accepted as a flash of understanding. The particulars of the concept of *pratibhā* are also expounded here in detail.

The third sections of *Vākyapadīya,* named as Padakāṇḍa or Prakīrṇakāṇḍa, is again divided into fourteen sections of *Vakyāpadīya* called Samuddeśas. As the name indicates, the discussions in this chapter are focused on the linguistic as well as philosophical analysis of words. The fourteen *samuddeśa*s are Jātisamuddeśa, Dravyasamuddeśa, Sambandhasamuddeśa, Dravyalakṣaṇasamuddeśa, Guṇasamuddeśa, Diksamuddeśa, Sādhanasamuddeśa, Kriyāsamuddeśa, Kālasamuddeśa, Puruṣasamuddeśa, Saṁkhyāsamuddeśa, Upagrahasamuddeśa, Liṅgasamuddeśa and Vr̥ttisamuddeśa.

COMMENTARIES OF VĀKYAPADĪYA

The text of *Vākyapadīya* has been commented upon by several scholars, but most of these commentaries are not available for the complete text. Ancient commentaries of the *Vākyapadīya* are available for several cantos of the text, while some later commentaries are up to the end of the text. Ancient commentaries include the *Vṛtti* by Harivṛṣabha, *Ṭīkā* of Puṇyarāja, *Paddhati* of Vṛṣabhadeva and commentary of Helārāja. There are some modern commentaries also, which emphasize on imparting a clear idea of the verses of *Vākyapadīya* for the students. A brief analysis of the commentaries of *Vākyapadīya* is given here.

Vṛtti

There is an old tradition, which says that Bhartṛhari himself had written a commentary on the *Vākyapadīya*, named *Vṛtti*. This is probably the oldest commentary available on the *Vākyapadīya*. I-tsing, the Chinese traveller, who visited India in 670 CE, recorded that Bhartṛhari had written a work containing 700 *kārikā*s and Bhartṛhari himself had written a commentary on it consisting 7,000 *kārikā*s. If so, the original commentary is in the form of *kārikā*s, but it is available in the form of prose commentary. In the commentary of Brahmakāṇḍa, the name of the author is found as Harivṛṣabha:

> *iti śrī harivṛṣabhamahāvaiyākaraṇaviracite vākyapadīye āgamasamuccayo nāma brahmakāṇḍaṁ samāptaṁ* ।
>
> – *Vākyapadīya* 2006: 236

Many scholars in Sanskrit explain the word *vṛṣabha* in praise of Hari (Bhartṛhari), just as Indra in Rājendra. This commentary is available for the first two *kāṇḍa*s. The commentary of first canto is available in full, but there are many gaps in that of the second canto.

The authorship of this commentary has been recently questioned by scholars like Ashok Aklujkar. He discusses the problem elaborately in his article titled "The Authorship of Vākyapadīya-Vṛtti" (1972). He sets forth many evidences to prove that the author of the *kārikā*s and that of the prose commentary are not the same

(1972: 181-98). Anyway, there is a scope for more authentic research to draw any conclusion in this regard.

Puṇyarāja

Puṇyarāja is believed to be born in Kashmir in the last decades of 800 CE. The details about the life of Puṇyarāja have not come to light fully. He himself says that he was known as Rājānakaśūravarma and studied the entire second canto of *Vākyapadīya* from Śaśāṅkaśiṣya (Limaye and Abhyankar 1965: 213). Vāmanācārya, who authored *Kāvyālaṁkārasūtra*, was known to be the disciple of Śaśāṅka. If Śaśāṅka, who is referred to by Puṇyarāja and the teacher of Vāmanācārya, is the same, then Puṇyarāja should be flourished after Vāmana, whose date is known to be 800 CE (Murti 1997: 13). These are the available details about the life of Puṇyarāja. But Murti holds that this information is subject to controversy.

Puṇyarāja wrote commentaries on the first and second cantos of *Vākyapadīya*. The first two cantos along with the *Ṭīkā* of Puṇyarāja have been published by Benares Sanskrit Series in 1884. But the available commentary on the first canto has many gaps in it and hence cannot be taken as complete. Fortunately, the *Ṭīkā* on the second canto including the *Vṛtti* of Harivṛṣabha is available in full. Peri Sarveswara Sharma is of the opinion that "the commentary on the first canto is an abridged version of Bhartṛhari's own *Vṛtti* and it is wrongly attributed to Puṇyarāja" (1972: 3).

Puṇyarāja has also composed a synopsis of the contents of the second canto of *Vākyapadīya* at the end of his commentary. He comprehends almost all the essential points of the second canto in 59 verses. The verses are written in a lucid style that the students and scholars can easily enter into the concepts of *Vākyapadīya*.

Helārāja

Helārāja has composed commentary on all the three cantos of *Vākyapadīya*, but his *Prakīrṇaprakāśa*, the commentary on the third canto, alone is extant now. In one of the introductory verses of his commentary on the third *kāṇḍa*, Helārāja says:

kāṇḍadvaye yathāvṛtti siddhāntārthasatattvataḥ |
prabandho vihito 'smabhirāgamārthānusāribhiḥ ||
– 7-8

Thus it is observed that he has written commentaries on the first two cantos. The commentary on the first *kāṇḍa* was named as *Śabdaprabhā*. Helārāja himself says:

vistareṇāgamaprāmāṇyam vākyapadīye 'smābhiḥ
prathamakāṇḍe śabdaprabhāyām nirṇītam | – 1994: 54

Aklujkar (1972: 193) holds that Helārāja's commentary on Brahmakāṇḍa was named as *Śabdaprabhā* and that on the second *kāṇḍa* as *Vākyakāṇḍaṭīkā* or *Vākyapradīpa*. References can be found that Helārāja composed another three works, viz. the *Advayasiddhi* (*Vākyapadīya* 1994: 117), *Kriyāviveka* (*Vākyapadīya* 1994: 60) and *Vārtikonmeṣa* (*Vākyapadīya* 1994: 149). But none of which is available now. Among these works, the *Vārtikonmeṣa*, as the name indicates, was an explanation of Kātyāyana's *Vārtika*s. The *Kriyāviveka* was intended to establish action (*kriyā*) as the main idea expressed by a sentence. The third, named *Advayasiddhi*, seems to have been a work on *śabdādvaita* (linguistic monism) (Coward and Raja 2008: 193).

A few references to the personal details of Helārāja can be found in his commentary *Prakīrṇaprakāśa*. Helārāja gives the following information about himself in the last portion of his commentary on Padakāṇḍa. He says:

muktāpīḍa iti prasiddhimagamat kāśmīradeśe nṛpaḥ
śrīmān khyātayaśā babhūva nṛpatestasya prabhāvānugaḥ
mantrī lakṣaṇa ityudāracaritastasyānvaye bhavo
helārāja imam prakāśamakarocchrī bhūtirājātmajaḥ |
– *Vākyapadīya* 3.14; Helārāja 1-2

> Helārāja, the son of Bhūtirāja, born in the family of Lakṣaṇa, who was a generous minister at the court of wealthy and famous Kashmiri king, popular with the name of Muktāpīḍa, composed this commentary called *Prakāśa*.

Abhinavagupta, who studied with Bhūtirāja, refers to the son of Bhūtirāja, whom he calls "Indurāja". Raja argues that Abhinavagupta refers to Helārāja in some passages as he is credited with having written a grammatical work named *Prakīrṇakavivaraṇa*. This is probably the commentary of *Vākyapadīya* by Helārāja known as *Prakīrṇaprakāśa* (Coward and Raja 2008: 193). It is evident that Kalhaṇa, in his famous work *Rājataraṅgiṇī*, refers to a king called Lalitāditya Muktāpīḍa, who lived in Kashmir at about 650–736 CE (2009: 130). Kalhaṇa also says that the king has many ministers in his court (2009: 144). Lakṣaṇa may have been one of these ministers. From these references, scholars conclude that Helārāja lived in the second half of the tenth century CE.

Helārāja's commentary on the third canto appears in the manuscripts sometimes asl the *Prakīrṇaprakāśa* and sometimes as the *Prakīrṇakaprakāśa*. Both may be deemed correct because the real name of the commentary is *Prakāśa* and *Prakīrṇa* or *Prakīrṇaka* is the name of the third canto of *Vākyapadīya*. While we go through the commentary, it can be found that Helārāja composed it according to the *Vr̥tti* of Bhartr̥hari. In the opening verse itself he says *yathāvr̥tti*, which means, this commentary is in accordance with the *Vr̥tti*. This makes the commentary more authentic. Several chapters in the Padakāṇḍa seem to be very difficult to understand as they deal with certain complicated philosophical as well as linguistic problems. Helārāja's commentary helps to have a vivid understanding of those complicated ideas. While going through the verses of Bhartr̥hari, sometimes we may get confused to determine Bhartr̥hari's own view, since he also quotes the views of others. In such situations, Helārāja distinguishes

Bhartṛhari's views from others. While explaining the concept of time (*kāla*) in Kālasamuddeśa, Bhartṛhari states that some call it as *śakti*, while others call it as *devatā* (*Vākyapadīya* III.7.62). Helārāja, commenting on this verse, opines that Bhartṛhari is of the view that time is power (*śakti*). To satisfy this, he refers to the third verse of the Brahmakāṇḍa which reads together with the *Vṛtti* There are some gaps in this commentary, so says Iyer. He says that all the manuscripts contain the indication of some scribe that the gaps have been filled up with the commentary of one Phullarāja (Introduction, 1974: 13-14).

Vṛṣabhadeva

A commentary of *Vākyapadīya* called *Paddhati* is attributed to Vṛṣabhadeva. He commented upon Bhartṛhari's *kārikā*s and the *Vṛtti* together. The *Paddhati* commentary also is available for the first canto only. From the introductory verses of the commentary, we may get some information about the author.

vimalacaritasya rājño viduṣaḥ śrī viṣṇuguptadevasya
bhṛtyena tadanubhāvācchridevayaśastanujena ।
bandhena vinodārthaṁ śrīvṛṣabheṇa sphuṭākṣaram nāma
kriyate paddhatireṣa vākyapadīyodadheḥ sugamā ॥
– *Paddhati* 1

It can be deduced from this verse that Vṛṣabhadeva was the son of Śrīdevayaśa, who was in the court of King Śrī Viṣṇuguptadeva. Vṛṣabhadeva mentions that there were many scholars who commented upon *Vākyapadīya* before him. Unfortunately, none of which is available now. According to Murti, Vṛṣabhadeva is supposed to have lived before the first half of eighth century CE (1997: 28). Again he opines that Vṛṣabhadeva had commented upon the first two cantos along with the *Vṛtti*, but the commentary on the second canto is not available. The style of commentary is lucid that even those who do not enter into the realm of grammar can understand the verses and the *Vṛtti* of *Vākyapadīya* by this commentary. This is probably the only ancient commentary available for the first canto, which follows the traditional style of commenting Śāstra works. The word *paddhati* in Sanskrit signifies path, way, manner, etc. Hence as the name indicates, this commentary pays a path to enter into the philosophical treatise *Vākyapadīya*.

Dravyesa Jha

Sanskrit grammarians consider the *Vākyapadīya* as authentic as the *Mahābhāṣya* of Patañjali. Hence this text has been included in the curriculum from old days. The verses of *Vākyapadīya* are so complicated that even the students of grammar are not able to understand the meaning easily. Hence some scholars have written commentaries to enter the students easily into the text. Dravyesa Jha, a famous scholar in Sanskrit grammar, composed a commentary *Pratyekārthaprakāśikā* on the first canto of *Vākyapadīya* in this dimension. This was published from Vrindavan in 1926. The commentary is only for the verses of *Vākyapadīya*, but not for the *Vṛtti*. While we go through the commentary, it can be noted that the author puts his mind on a brief meaning of each verse. He had no intentions to compose an elaborated commentary to untie the complicated issues which are conceived in the *kārikā*s of Bhartṛhari.

Suryanarayana Sukla

Bhāvapradīpa, a commentary on the Brahmakāṇḍa of *Vākyapadīya*, was written by Suryanarayana Sukla, which was published initially in 1937. Later it was published from Chaukhamba Sanskrit Sansthan, Varanasi, which has many editions also.

The author acknowledges his intention to write this commentary in the text as follows:

> *tasya paramopādeyatāmālocya tattatparikṣādhyakṣaiḥ vyākaraṇācārya parikṣāyām niveśitasya tasya yathārtham*

arthāvabodhāya saralavyākhyām anviṣyadbhiḥ chātraiḥ tadalābhena prārthitena mayā ।

vākyapadīyabhāvapradīpanāmnī vyākhyā viracayya viśveśvaracaraṇakamalayoḥ samarpya bhavatāṁ karakamalayoḥ upahārīkriyate ।

– Vākyapadīya 1937, Acknowledgement

We can understand from this passage that this commentary is also actually intended for the students to have a clear idea of the verses of *Vākyapadīya*. In a thorough evaluation, we can say that this is equally helpful for the scholars also. The commentator says about the nature of the commentary in the opening verse as:

pradīpasāhāyyam avāpya bhāṣyam
vigāhya tantrāntaram āgamāṁśca ।
vitanyate vākyapadīyabhāva-
pradīpa eṣo 'titarāmudāraḥ ॥

— Sukla 1

This verse shows that he wrote *Bhāvapradīpa* commentary, absorbing the views from the *Mahābhāṣya* of Patañjali along with the commentary *Pradīpa* by Kaiyaṭa as well as other *tantras* or schools of thought. He quotes from other texts also to give a clear idea of Bhartṛhari's verses, wherever necessary. While commenting upon the 31st *kārikā* of *Vākyapadīya*, Sukla quotes from the *Ślokavārtika*. In the same manner he refers to many other texts, which makes the commentary lucid as well as authentic.

Raghunatha Sarma

Raghunatha Sarma, a famous Sanskrit scholar not only in Grammar but in other schools of thought, wrote a commentary on the *Vākyapadīya*, which is equally praised by scholars and students. Probably this commentary, named *Ambākartrī* is the only commentary available for the whole text of *Vākyapadīya* along with the *Vṛtti*. In addition to this, he has included all the available authentic commentaries in his work. In the Introduction to this commentary on the first book of *Vākyapadīya*, Iyer describes that the present commentary is helpful for students as well as scholars (*Vākyapadīya* 2006: 11). All the three cantos of *Vākyapadīya* along with the commentary *Ambākartrī* have been published from Sampurnanand Sanskrit Vishwavidyalaya, Varanasi. The *Ambākartrī* commentary of the first canto of *Vākyapadīya* is published along with the *Svopajñavṛtti*, while the second canto is with the *Svopajñavṛtti* and *Ṭīkā* of Puṇyarāja and the third canto is with the *Prakīrṇaprakāśa* of Helārāja. Hence this edition can be taken as a complete reference about the text *Vākyapadīya*.

Sarma took sixteen years to complete his commentary *Ambākartrī* on the whole *Vākyapadīya*. He admits that he wrote commentary on the first book of *Vākyapadīya* by studying the verses and *Vṛtti* of Bhartṛhari and *Paddhati* commentary of Vṛṣabhadeva (Acknowledgement). Though Raghunatha Sarma admits that he follows the commentary of Vṛṣabhadeva, this commentary can be considered an independent work.

Vamadeva Acarya

Vamadeva Acarya wrote a commentary on the first canto of *Vākyapadīya*, which is named *Pratibhā*. This is a bilingual commentary both in Sanskrit and Hindi. This is a later commentary published in 1987 from Chaukhamba Sanskrit Sansthan, Varanasi. Apart from following the traditional way of commenting a Śāstra text, Vamadeva Acarya had a new approach to the *Vākyapadīya*. The text has an elaborate Preface, which expounds the ideas of Bhartṛhari in a new dimension.

K.A. Subramania Iyer

K.A. Subramania Iyer, a versatile scholar in more than one school of thought, has set forth original concepts on Bhartṛhari and the *Vākyapadīya*. He has critically edited all the three cantos of *Vākyapadīya* along with the authentic commentaries. The first canto of *Vākyapadīya* is edited with the *Vṛtti* and the ancient commentary *Paddhati* of Vṛṣabhadeva from Deccan College, Pune. The second canto is edited with the *Vṛtti* and *Ṭīkā* of Puṇyarāja, which has been published from Motilal Banarsidass, Delhi. He compiled and edited the third canto along with the *Prakāśa* commentary of Helārāja in two parts, which got published in Deccan College Series. He also translated all the three *kāṇḍa*s into English along with exegetical notes. Iyer gave a brief summary of the topics in each canto. He produced several original and authentic works in the studies of Bhartṛhari and the *Vākyapadīya*.

K. Raghavan Pillai

There are several scholars from Kerala, who have endeavoured in the studies of *Vākyapadīya* and Bhartṛhari. K. Raghavan Pillai, who had been the Director and Professor of Sanskrit in the Oriental Research Institute and Manuscripts Library, Kerala University for a long time, made notable contributions in this regard. He edited and translated the first two cantos of *Vākyapadīya* into English. Though several translations of the *Vākyapadīya* are available, this translation is unique in its rendition. In the present translation, each verse is preceded by an introduction and followed by summary, commentary and notes. Pillai himself states that this style of translation will be helpful for the readers to comprehend the main points of each verse. He acknowledges that the style of the translation is similar to the one rendered to a *śiṣya* by a *guru* in the traditional way. The translation consists of a brief but scholarly introduction, which is useful to both students and researchers.

M.H. Sastri

Some scholars from Kerala also have commented upon and translated *Vākyapadīya* into Malayalam. M.H. Sastri, who was a great scholar in more than one school of thought, wrote a commentary named *Hariharaputrīyam.* As the author says, he had an intention to write this commentary in Malayalam, but with the inspiration of some students, he decided to compose it in Sanskrit, English and Malayalam. The author's name was actually Hariharaputra and hence the work was named *Hariharaputrīyam.*

2

Perspectives on the Concept of Sentence in Indian Systems of Knowledge

Śabda: A Valid Source of Knowledge

As we know, the prime use of language (*śabda*) is communication. Daṇḍin, the famous rhetorician affirms that all the three worlds would be in blinding darkness unless the light called *śabda* had shone all around us (Daṇḍin 2005: 1.4). Usually *śabda* conveys information to the listeners hitherto unknown. Information, goods and whatever we wish to have, we gain them with the help of *śabda*. Thus, *śabda* makes human life possible. These are the probable implications of this verse. Here the face of language, which is used for communication, is unveiled. In communication, language is a signifier (*saṅketa*), which is popular in a society. In a particular society, certain meanings are assigned to a word and hence we should be familiar with those assignations (*saṅketa*) to communicate with the society. In this communicative level of language, words, which are the group of syllables, are only symbols of the meaning. This primary level of language is well said by Patañjali in the passage:

> *athavā pratītapadārthako loke dhvaniḥ śabda ityucyate*
> *tasmād* । *dhvaniḥ śabdaḥ* । – *Mahābhāṣya* 1984: 12

But before the utterance, the speaker conceives an idea, which is to be expressed and this is also considered as *śabda* by Sanskrit grammarians. We can trace this level of language also in the *Mahābhāṣya*, where Patañjali defines *śabda* as:

> *yenoccāritena sāsnālāṅgūlakakudakhuraviṣāṇināṁ sampratyayo bhavati sa śabdaḥ* – 1984: 11

In this passage, the term *sampratyaya* signifies the idea, which is manifested in the hearer's mind and is defined as *śabda*. Without these conceptions, an utterance could not be happened. At this point, language possesses a philosophical perspective. Hence we can analyse *śabda* (language) in two distinct perspectives, viz. from the point of view of communication and that of philosophy. Both the perspectives have attracted linguists as well.

Apart from mere communication, *śabda* unveils information that is not known to us, till it is uttered. Thus, *śabda* can be accepted as a source of valid knowledge. In Indian philosophy, Vaiśeṣikas and Cārvākas do not accept the validity of *śabda-pramāṇa*, arguing that it can be included in inference. While the preceptors of Nyāya and Mīmāṁsā accept *śabda* as a distinct *pramāṇa*, which is a source of valid knowledge. Naiyāyikas like Jayanta Bhaṭṭa, Jagadīśa and Gadādhara refute the arguments of Vaiśeṣikas and Cārvākas and put forth much logic to establish *śabda* as a different means of knowledge.

Grammarians give prime position to *śabda*, for their whole science is relied on it. This is evidently accepted by Patañjali as:

> *śabdapramāṇakā vayam, yacchabda āha tadasmākam pramāṇam* – *Mahābhāṣya* 1984: 56

Bhartṛhari, in accordance with Patañjali, accepts the superiority of *śabda* among the sources of valid knowledge. After establishing *śabda* as the essence of the whole world saying that it is word that form the basis of meaning, purposes, activities and truth (*Vākyapadīya* I.13). Bhartṛhari remarks that Vedas are the soul means of attaining this principle of language. Bhartṛhari presents a keen discussion about the authenticity of Vedas. Vedas are also in the form of *śabda* and hence the authenticity of *śabda* as a valid source of knowledge can be established.

Śabda-pramāṇa and Sentence

Śabda is accepted as a distinct *pramāṇa* by most of the schools of thought born and developed in India. Therefore, the followers of each school have to define *śabda* in accordance with their preconceptions. In general, philosophers use the term *śabda* to denote word as well as sentence. Gautama defines *śabda* in the aphorism *āptopadeśaḥ śabdaḥ* (*Nyāyadarśanam*, 1967: I.1.7), which says that *śabda* is that which is uttered by a trustworthy person. The commentators explain the characteristics of a trustworthy person. A trustworthy person is he, who has the knowledge of objects conducive to the attainment of what is beneficial and the avoidance of what is harmful. It is to be noted that the sentence uttered by the trustworthy person should consist of words having mutual expectancy (*ākāṅkṣā*), congruity (*yogyatā*) and proximity (*sannidhi*). Then only it can be accepted as a valid verbal testimony (*śabda-pramāṇa*). Thus the commentators interpret this aphorism, by elaborating the word *upadeśa* into the context of verbal testimony. The word *upadeśa* signifies the medium, through which something is communicated. It is generally accepted by almost all philosophers that sentence is the basic unit of communication, through which a complete idea hitherto unknown is communicated. Thus, the definitions of *śabda* by various philosophers can be applied only to sentence, neither to words nor to syllables. Mutual expectancy, congruity and proximity are the qualities of a sentence, but not of a word. Vācaspati Miśra in his commentary on *Nyāyavārtika*, clearly states that the word *upadeśa* denotes the cognition of sentence-meaning (*upadiśyate 'nena iti upadeśo vākyajñānam, – Nyāyadarśanam*, 1967: 173). Jagadīśa airs his idea about *śabda-pramāṇa* in the opening verse of *Śabdaśaktiprakāśikā*, a treatise on verbal testimony of the Nyāya school:

anubhavahetuḥ sakale sadyaḥ samupāsitā manuje ।
sākāṅkṣāsannā ca svārthe yogyā sarasvatī devī ॥

Goddess Sarasvatī is worshipped in this verse. Equivocally he refers to *śabda-pramāṇa*, which should be *sākāṅkṣam* (having mutual expectancy), *āsannam* (proximate) and *yogyam* (congruent). These characteristics of *śabda* obviously denote a sentence.

Gaṅgeśa defines *śabda-pramāṇa* in his *Tattvacintāmaṇi* 1 as:

atha śabdo nirūpyate । *prayogahetubhūtārthatattva-jñānajanyaḥ śabdaḥ pramāṇam* ।

According to him, the word, which is caused by the speaker's knowledge of facts and which causes an utterance of that word, only can be taken as *śabda-pramāṇa*.

In the *Tarkasaṁgraha*, Annambhaṭṭa defines *śabda* as: *āptavākyaṁ śabdaḥ* (1971: 65). He is also of the view that *śabda* is the sentence, uttered by a trustworthy person. Govardhana, while commenting on this statement, says that a trustworthy person is the person who has the knowledge of an object which is the cause of verbal expression (*Tarkasaṁgraha, Nyāyabodhinī* 1971: 65). In all these definitions, the word *śabda* is used in the technical sense of a sentence.

Mīmāṁsā philosophy contributed much in the scenario of *śābdabodha* (verbal cognition). This school admits the unquestioned authenticity of Vedas, which are in the form of *śabda*. Thus *śabda-pramāṇa* is one of the most important valid sources of knowledge in this philosophy. They also accept *śabda-pramāṇa* in the form of sentence. Śabara, the author of the *Bhāṣya* of *Mīmāṁsāsūtras*, opines that *śāstram śabdavijñānād asannikṛṣṭe 'rthe vijñānam* (under Jaimini I.1.5). He clarifies this statement saying:

> *yaḥ śabdaḥ svaviṣayakajñānena mānāntaraprāptābādhitārthajñānaṁ janayati sa pramāṇam* ।

That word, which is already known and gives rise to the cognition and that is not known by any other valid means of knowledge (*pramāṇa*) and also not contradicted subsequently, is known as *āśabda-pramāṇa*. Here, the word which gives rise to the cognition is also in the form of a sentence.

Vedānta also accepts *śabda-pramāṇa* as a distinct valid source of knowledge. Vedāntadeśika defines *śabda-pramāṇa* as *anāptānuktavākyam śabdaḥ* (quoted in Tatacharya 2005: 9). According to this definition, the sentence, which is not uttered by an untrustworthy person, is the valid source of knowledge. In this statement, he uses two negatives *na*, to affirm that the sentence uttered by a trustworthy person only should be considered as authentic. Thus, it can be applied to both Vedas, which are not uttered by anyone as well as secular statements, uttered by a trustworthy person. While in his *Vedāntaparibhāṣā*, Dharmarāja Adhvarin puts forth a different opinion:

> *yasya vākyasya tātparyaviṣayībhūtaḥ saṁsargaḥ mānāntareṇa na bādhyate tad vākyaṁ pramāṇam iti* ।
>
> – 1985: 208

Here, the sentence, which gives rise to a valid cognition of the relation between the words and is not cancelled by any other *pramāṇa* subsequently, is accepted as the valid source of knowledge. In both the definitions, the term *vākya* is used and hence they also admit the authenticity of *śabda*. Hence, it can be concluded that almost all Indian schools of thought, who accept *śabda-pramāṇa*, accept it in the form of sentence.

Defining Sentence: Various Views

It is observed here that Indian philosophies have given *śabda* a prime position in their metaphysic and epistemology. Technically speaking, philosophies like Mīmāṁsā and Nyāya as well as the school of Vyākaraṇa have contributed much to the analysis of the concept of *śabda*. They have analysed words, sentences and their meaning in a scientific way. In addition to this, they have also discussed various philosophical as well as linguistic problems regarding words, sentences and their meaning.

Since these schools of thought accept *śabda* in the form of sentence as one among the *pramāṇa*s, they have tried to define sentence in their own perspectives. Ancient texts of Indian philosophy have discussed about the concepts of *vāk*, *śabda*, etc. but none of them specifically defines a sentence. A reference can be seen in the *Bṛhaddevatā* that a sentence is the *saṁghāta* (collection of words) (*padasaṅghātajam vākyam* – 2.117). Amarasiṁha gives two definitions of sentence: as a group of verbs and nouns and as a verb, which is connected with *kāraka*s:

suptiṅantacayo vākyaṁ kriyā vā kārakānvitā । – 1.6.2

Later, many scholars in different branches of knowledge have tried to define sentence in manifold ways according to their perspectives. This chapter tries to converge various views on the concept of sentence and sentence-meaning in Indian systems of knowledge.

SENTENCE ACCORDING TO THE MĪMĀṀSĀ SCHOOL

Mīmāṁsā is the oldest system among the Indian schools of thought that tries to define a sentence. As stated, an early simple definition is seen in the *Bṛhaddevatā*, one of the ancient works in Mīmāṁsā (2.117). It is in the *Mīmāṁsāsūtras* of Jaimini that we first come across the real definition of a sentence. He states that *arthaikatvād ekaṁ vākyaṁ sākāṅkṣaṁ cedvibhāge syāt* (2.1.46), which can be explained as a group of words serving a single purpose forms a sentence, if on analysis, the separate words are found to have *ākāṅkṣā* (mutual expectancy). Kunjunni Raja opines that the Mīmāṁsakas enunciate this principle so as to deal with the passages of the *Yajurveda* (1963: 152). Śabara also explains this aphorism as referring to the Vedic *mantra*s only, and the term *arthaikatva* is interpreted in the sense of serving a single purpose:

> *yāvanti padāni ekaṁ prayojanam abhinirvartayanti tāvanti padāni ekaṁ vākyam* । – Under Jaimini 2.2.26

Though Jaimini coined this definition for explaining the Vedic sentences, it is capable of much more extended application. Bhartṛhari reiterates this as one of the well-known definitions of sentence.

> *sākāṅkṣāvayavam bhede parānākāṅkṣaśabdakam* ।
> *karmapradhānam guṇavadekārtham vākyamiṣyate* ॥
> – *Vākyapadīya* II.4

Kumārila also sets forth the same view that sentence is a group of words. He says: it must be concluded that those words on hearing which we are clearly cognizant of a single idea, must be regarded as one sentence, either ordinary or of the *mantra* and *brāhmaṇa* (*Tantravārtika*, 1929: 586). He explains the word *arthaikatva* in the aphorism in the sense of single idea. Among his followers, Pārthasārathi Miśra favours the view of Śabara and explains the word *artha* in the sense of "purpose" (Jha 1942: 190). Someśwara Bhaṭṭa in his *Nyāyasudhā* commentary takes the term in the sense of "meaning" to admit a wider scope of the definition (1982: 681). Śālikanātha refers to Prabhākara's view in his *Prakaraṇapañcikā*. Here, it states that a sentence is a group of words:

> *padānyeva vākyam* । *padārthā eva vākyārtha iti gurumatasthitiḥ* । – 1961: 377

Ganganatha Jha argues that according to Prabhākara, the word *artha* in the definition of Jaimini stands for "meaning" as well as "purpose", for both are interrelated. He says that the words of a sentence must be related to the purpose, which is the most important factor in a sentence (1942: 190). If we analyse these definitions, it may be noted that, like the Naiyāyikas, Mīmāṁsakas also accept the group of words as a sentence. But they lay stress on the necessity of *ākāṅkṣā* (syntactic expectancy) among the words, in order to bring about the unity of idea or of purpose. Kunjunni Raja refers to some of the definitions of sentence found in Śrautasūtras, and he states that those definitions are based on the Mīmāṁsā views (1963: 154).

Mīmāṁsakas do not admit a sentence as distinct from words and words as distinct from letters. Śabara refers to Upavarṣa, who says that the word *gau* is constituted by the letters *g*, *au* and *visarjanīya*. Thus, syllables are comprehended by the sense of hearing and not anything different from it (quoted in Tatacharya 2005: 15). Śabara then explains how the letters attain the status of a word. The last syllable associated with the latent impressions, born out of the cognitions of each preceding syllable, gives rise to the cognition of the word-meaning. In the same way the last word associated with the latent impressions of each word gives rise to sentence-meaning.

Mīmāṁsakas refute the *sphoṭa* theory and the concept of indivisibility of the sentence formulated by the grammarians. But they maintain that the articulate phonemes are eternal. Tatacharya summarizes the view of Mīmāṁsakas as, *śabda* is none other than the articulated syllables and the syllables eternal. They are associated together to form words and sentences.

> *śrotragrāhyā varṇā eva śabdaḥ* । *teṣāmeva vācakatvam-arthapratyāyakatvam* । *te kaṇṭhatālvādyabhighātavyaṅgyāḥ nityā vibhavaśca* । *ta eva varṇāḥ samuditāḥ padavākyavyapadeśabhājo'rthapratyāyakā ityāhuḥ* । – Tatacharya 2005: 115

Thus, the Mīmāṁsakas admit the articulate phonemes are eternal, while the grammarians accept the eternity of sound in the form of sentence.

SENTENCE ACCORDING TO THE NYĀYA SCHOOL

Gautama, in his *Nyāyadarśana*, refers to the word *vākya* in the aphorism *vākyavibhāgasya cārthagrahaṇāt* (2.1.161). But no precise definition of sentence is formulated by him. Vātsyāyana, in his commentary on the aphorism 2.1.54, states that a sentence consists of several units in the form of two or more words. Thus he considers sentence as that which is consisting of a group of words. Jayanta Bhaṭṭa makes his opinion that the absence of any reference to the sentence in the *Nyāyasūtras* shows that the early Naiyāyikas treated the sentence to be merely a combination of words:

> *kiṁ punaridaṁ padaṁ nāma, kiṁ ca vākyam iti uktam atra varṇasamūhaḥ padaṁ padasamūho vākyamiti*
>
> – Jayanta Bhaṭṭa 1970: 143

Vācaspati Miśra states that *varṇa*s (syllables) constitute a word and the collection of words denotes a sentence. He also opines that the semantic relation among word-meanings has been comprehended to give rise to the recollection of their meaning and then to the sentence-meaning which is unknown hitherto:

> *tasmāt padāni kr̥tasaṅketāni svārthaṁ smārayitvā ākāṅkṣā-yogyatā-āsatti-sādhrīcīnāni adr̥ṣṭapūrvaṁ vākyārthaṁ bodhayanti* ।
>
> – 1967: 178

Later scholars in Nyāya consider sentence as not a mere combination of words, but a group of words possessing *ākāṅkṣā*, *yogyatā* and *sannidhi*.

Among the later scholars, Keśava Miśra gives a vivid description about the nature of sentence in his *Tarkabhāṣā*. He defines sentence as the group of words possessing three qualities, viz. *ākāṅkṣā* (verbal expectancy), *yogyatā* (congruity) and *sannidhi* (proximity):

> *vākyaṁ tu ākāṅkṣāyogyatāsannidhimatāṁ padānāṁ samūhaḥ* ।
> – *Tarkabhāṣya* 1995: 121

Thus he says that a mere combination of words like *gauḥ, aśvaḥ, puruṣaḥ, hastī,* etc. cannot be called a sentence, for it lacks verbal expectancy. Similarly the sentences like *vahninā siñcati* (spray with fire) is also not an authentic sentence as it lacks congruity. Fire cannot be taken as an instrument for the act of spraying. Similarly if one says the word *gām* and after a long interval, he says *ānaya*, it will not form a sentence because of the absence of proximity. Thus, he mentions that sentence is a group of words, which have these peculiarities:

i. Words produce the verbal expectancy in the listener's mind through the denotation of their meanings.
ii. They convey meanings that are capable of being connected without contradiction.
iii. They are close enough to produce the intended meaning without undue delay (*arthapratipādanadvārā śrotuḥ padāntaraviṣayāṁ vākāṅkṣāṁ janayatāṁ, pratīyamāna-parasparānvaya-yogyatārtha-pratipādakānāṁ, sannihitānāṁ padānāṁ samūho vākyam*). – Ibid.: 125

When compared to the old school of Nyāya, the Neo-Logicians (Navya-Naiyāyikas) have special interest in the concept of language and language analysis. L.C. Mullatti argues in his thesis "The Navya-Nyāya Theory of Inference" that the Neo-Logicians gave much importance to sentences because of their special interest in the extralinguistic entities, namely, cognitions.

> There was, in fact, an important reason, for the Navya Naiyāyikas' interest in sentences. Though they did not realise it, they were

> inevitably faced with the problem of individuation of the extra-linguistic entities they allowed, namely, cognitions. Lacking any other principle of individuation, they were forced to rely on linguistic considerations. – 1972: 40

This special emphasis on the concept of sentence and its analysis can be evidently seen in the works of Neo-Logicians.

Udayana in his *Nyāyakusumāñjali*, one of the major works in the Navya-Nyāya school, affirms that sentence is only a group of words. He also states that the group of words is not different from the words, which are its constituents. It is also known to him that words, which do not have the syntactic expectancy (*ākāṅkṣā*), congruity (*yogyatā*) and proximity (*sannidhi*), do not constitute a sentence or verbal testimony (5.6). Another major work in this school, *Tattvacintāmaṇi* of Gaṅgeśa too explains the nature of sentence as the group of words and it constitutes the cause of verbal cognition. He states that the words are the instrumental cause (*kāraṇa*), the recollection of word-meaning is the intermediate cause (*vyāpāra*), the syntactic expectancy, etc. are the auxiliary cause (*sahakārikāraṇa*) and the experience (*anubhava*) of the relation among the recollected word-meanings on the strength of the auxiliary cause is the fruit:

> *tasmāt padam karaṇaṁ, padārthasmaraṇaṁ vyāpāraḥ, ākāṅkṣādisahakārivaśāt smāritārthānvayānubhavaḥ phalam* । – *Tattvacintāmaṇi* 1990: 548

A statement from the *Tattvacintāmaṇi* is referred to in the work *Nyāyakośa* as follows:

> *vākyaṁ padasamūhaḥ* । *vākyatvaṁ ca viśiṣṭārtha-paraśabdatvam* । – *Nyāyakośa* 1928: 730

It says that a sentence is a group of words; and the state of a sentence lies in giving rise to the cognition of the relation among the word-meanings.

The *Śabdaśaktiprakāśikā* of Jagadīśa is one of the major works in Navya-Nyāya, which specially focuses on the language theory of Naiyāyikas. He elaborately discusses on the nature of sentence. According to him, sentence is a group of words having mutual syntactic expectancy (*ākāṅkṣā*), etc. and which is conducive to give rise to a unified awareness of the connected meanings of the words:

> *athavā yādr̥śaśabdānāṁ yādr̥śārthaviṣayakabodhaṁ pratyanukūlā parasparākāṅkṣā, tādr̥śaśabdastoma eva tathāvidhārthe vākyam* ı – 2002: 12

Annambhaṭṭa also says that a word is that which have a semantic potential and a sentence is a group of such words:

> *śaktaṁ padam* ı *vākyaṁ padasamūhaḥ* ı
> – *Tarkasaṁgraha* 1971: 151

Thus it can be concluded that Naiyāyikas accept sentence as a group of words having syntactic expectancy, congruity and proximity.

According to them, the collective form is not different from its units or parts and therefore a sentence is not different from the articulated alphabets. But how the articulated alphabets can be perceived as a sentence is the problem to be solved. Vātsyāyana tries to explain how the sentence is not distinct from the phonemes:

> *vākyastheṣu khalu varṇeṣūccaratsu prativarṇam tāvat śravaṇaṁ bhavati* ı *śrutaṁ varṇamekamanekaṁ vā padabhāvena pratisandhatte* ı *pratisandhāya padaṁ vyavasyati* ı *sambaddhāṁśca padārthān gr̥hītvā vākyārthaṁ pratipadyate* ı
> – *Nyāyadarśana, Nyāyabhāṣya* 3.2.59

It is Jayanta Bhaṭṭa who discusses the matter elaborately in his *Nyāyamañjarī*. He says that initially, the cognition of the first phoneme is awakened and it is followed by its latent impression. Then the cognition of the second phoneme, followed by its latent impression takes place. In this manner, the latent impressions are awakened till the cognition of the last phoneme. In the end, when the last phoneme is heard, there occurs a single recollection comprehending all the phonemes and is the word. In the same way, there takes place the cognition of the first word followed by its latent impression and by the recollection of its significative relation to its meaning simultaneously. Thus the word-meaning is also cognized, followed by its latent impression. The same continues till the cognition of the last word. Thus due to the previous latent impressions, a recollection comprehending all the words is occurred and is the sentence. There happens another recollection based upon the latent impressions of all the word-meanings comprehending the meaning of the last word and is the sentence-meaning (6.2). Similar view can be seen in *Nyāyalīlāvatī* also as:

> *kiṁ tarhi prātipadikam? kramavadvarṇasaṁhatiriti brūmaḥ* । – Quoted in Tatacharya 2005: 115

Naiyāyikas, in contradiction with grammarians, do not accept the eternity of *śabda*. They refute the theory of *sphoṭa* and the theory of sentence indivisibility, formulated by grammarians. Gautama refutes the view of *śabda-nityatva* saying that *śabda* is not eternal, as it has a beginning and an end:

> *ādimatvāt-aindriyakatvāt kr̥takatvāt-upacārācca*
> – *Nyāyadarśnam* 2.2.13

As described, logicians accept sentence as an aggregate of phonemes. According to them, word is the meaningful unit of language (*śaktam padam* । – *Tarkasaṁgraha* 1971: 151). They refute the theory of *sphoṭa* and the theory of indivisibility of sentence because they hold that a word or a sentence becomes the source of valid knowledge when it is uttered by a trustworthy person. *Sphoṭa*, being eternal, does not owe its existence to a trustworthy person (Sharma 1998: 80).

SENTENCE ACCORDING TO THE SCHOOL OF VYĀKARAṆA

In the science of grammar, the early preceptors Pāṇini, Kātyāyana and Patañjali, also known as *trimuni*, pointed out some aspects of sentence in their works. Pāṇini has not given a vivid definition of sentence in his monumental work *Aṣṭādhyāyī*. But there are two occasions, where Pāṇini hinted his views on sentence. He refers to the term *vākya* in the aphorism *vākyasya ṭeḥ pluta udāttaḥ* (VIII.2.82). The whole idea of Pāṇini about sentence can be traced in the aphorism *samarthaḥ padavidhiḥ* (II.1.1).

Usually, Mīmāṁsakas are considered to be the first to promulgate the necessity of *ākāṅkṣā* among the meanings of the words in a sentence in order to bring about the unity of idea. But the necessity for interdependence of words to give a unified meaning was recognized even earlier by Pāṇini, who conceived the concept of *ākāṅkṣā* by the word *samartha* (*samarthaḥ padavidhiḥ* – 2.1.1). This term has been variously interpreted by the commentators of Pāṇini. Patañjali states that according to some, the word *sāmarthya* denotes *vyapekṣā* (mutual connection) pertaining to the meaning (*parasparavyapekṣāṁ sāmarthyameke* – *Mahābhāṣya* 1991: 365). This interpretation is similar to the concept of *ākāṅkṣā* given by the Mīmāṁsakas. Kātyāyana explains the term *sāmarthya* as *ekārthībhāva* (unification of meaning) (*pṛthagarthānām ekārthībhavaḥ sāmarthyam* – under Pāṇini II.1.1). This implies the capability of words to make compounds in which, different words with different meanings are infused together to signify a unified meaning. This explanation of the term *sāmarthya* seems analogous to the condition of *arthaikatva* formulated by Jaimini, if it is interpreted as unity of meaning (Raja 1963: 155). Here Pāṇini intends to say that the words are capable of forming either a sentence or a compound. When words possess *ekārthībhāvasāmarthya* (capability of giving a unified sense), they could make compound words, losing their individual meanings and acquire a special signification. Similarly, when the words possess *vyapekṣārūpasāmarthya*, they could make sentences, in which they retain their own meanings, but are mutually related. Commentators like Kaiyaṭa are of this opinion; he says:

> *iha vyapekṣāyām samāso na bhavati, ekārthībhāve vākyaṁ neti* । – *Mahābhāṣya*, under Pāṇini II.1.1

Haradatta, in his work *Padamañjarī*, states that both *ekārthībhāva* and *vyapekṣā* are necessary in a compound word, because in the absence of mutual connection of meanings, words are not allowed to form a compound (under Pāṇini II.1.1). We can infer from these discussions that Pāṇini has summarized all his ideas about sentence in the word *samartha*.

In Sanskrit grammar, it was Kātyāyana, who did the first attempt to define a sentence. Patañjali remarks:

> *idam adyāpūrvam kriyate vākyasaṁjñā samānavākyādhikāraśca* । – *Mahābhāṣya,* under Pāṇini II.1.1

Some scholars hold that because of this reason, Kātyāyana was also known as *vākyakāra* (Jha 2002: 5). Kātyāyana defines sentence in two perspectives as *ekatiṅvākyam* and *ākhyātaṁ sāvyayakārakaviśeṣaṇaṁ vākyam* (under Pāṇini II.1.1). The former definition states that sentence is that which has one finite verb. But this definition is somewhat absurd in nature. There are obviously sentences having more than one finite verb like *paśya mr̥go dhāvati* (behold, the animal runs). Later grammarians accept this as a single sentence as it gives a unified sense. Thus Kaiyaṭa interprets this definition in a different perspective as *ekaḥ, samānaḥ tiṅ yasmin tat ekatiṅ* (under Pāṇini II.1.1). Thus, from the formal surface level approach, such a sentence may be considered as a complex one made up of two simple sentences. But at the deep structure level, it has a semantic unity and thus it is considered as a single sentence. Thus Kātyāyana proposes the latter definition. According to this, there is only one verb in a sentence, the meaning of which is the primary substantive (*viśeṣya*) and the other words (including verbs) are adjectives (*viśeṣaṇa*) of the main verb. Thus in the above sentence, though there are two verbs, the meaning of the one (*paśya*) is the primary substantive and the meaning of the other (*dhāvati*) is only its attribute (*viśeṣaṇa*).

SENTENCE ACCORDING TO OTHER SCHOOLS

The subdivisions of the school of Vedānta, viz. Advaita, Viśiṣṭādvaita and Dvaita, also deny the eternity of *śabda*, advocated by Bhartṛhari and the concept of *sphoṭa*. Though any of these schools does not emphasize the concept of language and language analysis in the technical discussions, some glimpses can be found in several works of these schools. Advaitins admit that letters, the objects of recollection, which results from the latent impressions born out of each letter, is the word or sentence. Śaṅkara states that the letters generate the notion of a word, thanks to their definite sequence (under *Brahmasūtra* 1.3.28). This school also admits the necessity of syntactic expectancy, etc. of words in a sentence. The Viśiṣṭādvaitins as well as Dvaitins also accept the same view as of Śaṅkara. According to them, letters constitute a word and the words constitute a sentence (Tatacharya 2005: xxx).

The Sāṁkhya system, like the Naiyāyikas, views a sentence as the group of words and a word as the group of phonemes. The followers of this school reject the *sphoṭa* theory of the grammarians:

> *pratītyapratītibhyām na sphoṭātmakaḥ śabdaḥ* ।
> – *Sāṁkhyasūtra* 5.57

Also they reject the theory of eternity of letters, advocated by the Mīmāṁsakas:

> *na śabdanityatvam kāryatāpratīteḥ* । – *Sāṁkhyasūtra* 5.58

In the Yoga system, the nature of sentence is explained in the aphorism:

śabdārthapratyayānāmitaretarādhyāsāt saṅkaraḥ-tatpravibhāgasamyamāt sarvabhūtarutajñānam ।
– *Pātañjalayogsūtraṇī* 1904: 3.17

According to this aphorism, the letters are uttered in a particular order and they become the content of a single cognition and thus constitute a single unit, word. Though the word is manifested by the final letter along with the latent impressions of previous letters, it does not have any reference to the sequence of letters. Thus the Yoga school accepts the nature of sentence similar to that of grammarians (Tatacharya 2005: xxxiii).

Nature of Sentence-Meaning: Various Perspectives

Most of the Indian schools of thought admit that a sentence is composed of words. They also accept that words have the potentiality of expressing definite meanings. When they are connected together, a single cognition is awakened and is the sentence-meaning. The preceptors of various branches of learning have been enquiring this relation among the words in a sentence and their meanings, through which they are semantically connected to give a unified sense. This resulted in various theories regarding the cognition of the meaning of a sentence and is generally called theories of *śābdabodha* (verbal cognition).

If these theories of verbal cognition advocated by various philosophers are analysed, two distinct perspectives on the concept of *śābdabodha* can be found. They are *khaṇḍa-śābdabodha* (import by parts) and *akhaṇḍa-śābdabodha* (unitary import). In the first perspective, the import is produced by parts. Here, each word in the sentence is analysed on the basis of its attributives like *kartṛtva* and *karmatva*. The Akhaṇḍa school of *śābdabodha* implies the verbal import of the sentence as opposed to that by parts. Here, the entire meaning of the sentence is conveyed and thus in most of the Śāstra works, the term *śābdabodha* refers only to the unitary import (Rao 1969: 4).

MĪMĀṀSAKAS' VIEW ON SENTENCE-MEANING

Mīmāṁsakas generally maintain that sentence-meaning is the word-meaning related to another word-meaning. Śabara states that sentence-meaning is the aggregate of the meanings of its parts. He emphasizes that sentence-meaning is neither without any basis, nor is based upon the significative relation (under Jaimini 1.1.7). Again he stresses upon the point that sentence-meaning is not the significance of words. Thus, a word-meaning, which is not related to another word-meaning, does not constitute the sentence-meaning (under Jaimini 3.2.1.1). According to him, a word conveys the universal (*sāmānya*) while a sentence conveys a particular (*viśeṣa*) (under Jaimini 1.1.24). This statement is explained in *Bṛhatī* as: a sentence conveys a particular, because of the interconnection of word-meanings. The state of words, which are not connected to each other, is universal (under Jaimini 1.1.24). When isolated, a word signifies its meaning, which is universal in nature. For example, when one says *śuklām gāṁ ānaya*, the word *śuklām* in isolation signifies the white colour, which is universal. Similarly the word *gām* in isolation denotes a cow, which is not characterized by its colour. When these words come together to form a sentence they lose their universal significance and denote a connected sense, which is particular. Śabara repeats the same view in several contexts in his commentary:

> *viśiṣṭārthasaṁpratyayaśca vākyārthaḥ* |
>
> – Under Jaimini 1.1.25
>
> *padārthaiḥ saṁskṛtaḥ piṇḍitaḥ arthaḥ vākyārthaḥ* |
>
> – 1.1.8.32

The conclusive view of Śabara on sentence-meaning is that, the meanings of words, which are universal in nature, when connected together, give the sentence-meaning, which is particular. Thus the meaning of a sentence is none other than *saṁsarga* (interconnection) of its constituent words.

In the *Tantravārtika*, it is stated that:

ākṛtipadārthapakṣe śuklatva-gotvayoḥ svarūpeṇa abhihitayoḥ sannidhānāt itaretarānurañjanam arthasidhabhedam vākyārthaḥ । – 2.1.14.46

Here, the word *itaretarānurañjanam* refers to *saṁsarga* (interconnection of words). Śālikanātha describes the nature of sentence-meaning from the point of view of Prabhākara. He states that a sentence is the collection of words and the word-meanings together constitute the sentence-meaning. But it is to be noted that one word-meaning is primary and when it is associated with the meanings of the other words in a sentence, which are secondary, gives the sentence-meaning (Tatacharya 2005: 25).

After hearing the words in a sentence, the listener manifests a unitary sense, by the mutual association of word-meanings. Here, it may be doubted that, whether this unitary sense is manifested directly from the collection of the words, or indirectly through the recollection of the meanings of the individual words that comprises it. These two views give rise to two theories of explaining the comprehension of the meaning of a sentence, viz. *anvitābhidhāna* and *abhihitānvaya* theories. The Prābhākara school of Mīmāṁsā and its followers take the former view, while the Bhāṭṭa school of Mīmāṁsā and some of the Naiyāyikas accept the *abhihitānvaya* theory of verbal comprehension.

ABHIHITĀNVAYA AND ANVITĀBHIDHĀNA THEORIES OF SENTENCE-MEANING

If every word has its own definite meaning, how is it possible for a sentence, which is only a collection of words, to have a unified meaning? The same problem arises in the case of compound words also (Raja 1963: 191). At this point, various philosophers hold different theses. Bhartṛhari presents his views on these theories by presenting the Vākyavādin–Padavādin controversy discussed in the second canto of *Vākyapadīya*. Among them, Abhihitānvayavāda and Anvitābhidhānavāda are the most important theories. These two views explain how a sentence is imported to cognize the meaning of it.

Abhihitānvaya Theory

According to this theory, each word in a sentence expresses a complete meaning, which can be comprehended separately. When a sentence is heard, the listener first understands the separate meanings of the words one after the other. The isolated word-meanings, expressed successively by the words, are put together by the collective memory of the listener which is termed as *samūhālaṁbana-smṛti.* The individual word-meanings are remembered separately until all the words are heard. Then the simultaneous cognition of the sentence-meaning takes place by putting together these word-meanings according to three factors, viz. *ākāṅkṣā*, *yogyatā* and *sannidhi*. The listeners can cognize the meaning of the sentence by this process. Thus, the followers of this theory advocate that the meaning of a sentence is a concatenation of the individual meanings expressed by its parts (Raja 1963: 203).

Kunjunni Raja suggests that this theory is deep-rooted in the views of the great grammarian Vājapyāyana and thus it is one of the earliest theories about the nature of sentence-meaning. Vājapyāyana advocates that the meaning of the sentence is *saṁsarga* (mutual association) of the individual word-meanings (Raja 1963: 205). Abhihitānvayavādins argue that Śabara seems to refer to this theory when he says:

> *padāni hi svaṁ svam artham abhidāya nivṛttavyāpārāṇi, athedānīṁ padārthāvagataḥ santo vākyārthaṁ gamayanti* ।
> – Under Jaimini 1.1.25

In a sentence, words cease to function after expressing their own meanings. Then the meanings of the words, thus known, give rise to the sentence-meaning. Kumārila Bhaṭṭa, the founder of the Bhāṭṭa school propagated this theory by giving it an important role in his philosophy. He affirms that the meaning of the sentence is always conveyed by the meanings of the words expressed by the individual words:

padārthaiḥ padavijñātaiḥ vākyārthaḥ pratipādyate
– *Ślokavārtika* 1983: 445

According to him, a sentence cannot signify a meaning, independent of its parts. Words in a sentence first express their meaning independently and then the connection among these word-meanings is established. This leads to the cognition of sentence-meaning and the three requisites, *ākāṅkṣā*, *yogyatā* and *sannidhi*, constitute the grounds of relationship among word-meanings (Ibid.: 455).

Many preceptors rightly observe that the sentence-meaning is something more than the sum of the individual word-meanings. Patañjali is in favour of this view, when he states:

yadatrādhikyam vākyārthaḥ saḥ । – *Mahābhāṣya* 1991: 462

Bhartṛhari also explains the nature of sentence-meaning in a similar manner:

saṁbandhe sati yattvanyadādhikyam upajāyate ।
vākyārthameva taṁ prāhuranekapadasaṁśrayam ॥
– *Vākyapadīya* II.42

Mammaṭa Bhaṭṭa describes this view vividly in his *Kāvyaprakāśa*. He says that when the meanings of different words in a sentence are related with one another on the basis of mutual expectancy, etc. some additional signification is known, which is distinct from the totality of the separate word-meanings.

> *ākāṅkṣāyogyatāsannidhivaśāt padārthānāṁ samanvaye tātparyārtho viśeṣavapurapadārtho 'pi vākyārthaḥ samullasatīti abhihitānvayavādināṁ matam* ।
>
> – *Kāvyaprakāśa* 2.6

This additional meaning is called by various names such as *vākyārtha*, *saṁsarga* and *tātparyārtha.*

How is this *saṁsarga* conveyed? Where does this additional meaning come from? These vexed questions need to be explained to understand the *abhihitānvaya* theory better. The individual words are not capable to convey the special signification, for they cease to function after expressing their individual meanings. Between the words and sentence-meaning, there lie the word-meanings and, thus, word-meanings convey the sentence-meaning in the form of *saṁsarga*. This view of Abhihitānvayavādins is well explained in the *Mānameyodaya* (93). The followers of Bhāṭṭa school claim that sentence-meaning is conveyed by the secondary power of words:

> *vākyārtho lakṣyamāṇo hi sarvatraiveti naḥ sthitiḥ* ।
>
> – Kumārila Bhaṭṭa, quoted in *Tattvabindu* 1936: 153

Naiyāyikas also admit the theory of *abhihitānvaya*, with slight differences. But according to them, the sentence-meaning is only the mutual relation of word-meanings. Navya-Naiyāyikas like Udayana and Gaṅgeśa reject the *anvitābhidhāna* point of view and advocate the *abhihitānvaya* theory of verbal cognition. But this view differs slightly from that of Kumārila. According to them, the word-meanings do not constitute the cause of verbal cognition, but the words alone constitute such a cause. The words give rise to the recollection of their meanings, which, owing to *ākāṅkṣā*, get themselves related to one another and the relation is the sentence-meaning (*Nyāyakusumāñjali* 1980: 216; *Tattvacintāmaṇi* 1990: 548-49). Jayanta examines both the views of verbal comprehension in his *Nyāyamañjarī* and records two views, viz. *anvīyamānābhidhāna* and *abhidhīyamānānvaya*. Rejecting these two views, he sets forth his own view as: the words in a sentence convey their meanings and the words have the power of conveying the meaning of the sentence also, which is known as *tātparya* (*Nyāyamañjarī* 6.2). It is to be noted here that the cognition of specific relation of one word-meaning to another (*tātparya*) cannot be treated as verbal. Advaita Vedānta also admits the theory of *abhihitānvaya*. Śaṅkara in his *Bhāṣya* on the *Brahmasūtra*, expresses his preference to this theory (under *Brahmasūtra* I.1.4). It is clear from the discussions that almost all systems of thought, except the Prābhākara school of Mīmāṁsā and Vaiyākaraṇas, accept this view of comprehending sentence-meaning.

Anvitābhidhāna Theory

As stated, this theory is held by the followers of the Prābhākara school of Mīmāṁsā. When a speech act is carried out, both the speaker and the listener are concerned with the meaning of the sentence, and not with the meanings of individual word-meanings. Thus Prabhākara opines that words do not convey a meaning except in the context of a sentence. Like the Abhihitānvayavādins, this school also upholds that the meaning of a sentence is cognized by the individual word-meanings and their mutual relation. But, what is peculiar to this view is that, the individual word-meanings and their relation are conveyed by the words themselves. They assert that it is impossible to comprehend the isolated meaning of a word apart from its relation in a sentence. The words convey their meanings only as related to one another in a sentence. Thus, each word denotes a connected meaning, and not its individual meaning, in the sentence. The Anvitābhidhānavādins admit that the words are capable to convey its meaning as well as the relation. Hence, the sentence-meaning is directly conveyed by the words themselves.

> *ākāṅkṣāsannidhiprāptayogyārthāntarasaṅgatān* ।
> *svārthān āhuḥ padānīti vyutpattiḥ saṁśritā mayā* ॥
> – *Vākyārthamātṛkāvṛtti*, quoted in Raja 1963: 98

This is the central idea of the theory of *anvitābhidhāna* propounded by Prabhākara and his followers.

This can be well explained by an example. In the sentence *gāmānaya* (bring the cow), the word "cow" does not denote an isolated meaning of "cowness". But it signifies the cow, which is related to the action of bringing. Similarly, the word "bring" does not signify the action of bringing in general, but related to the cow. Thus the words in this sentence express their own meaning, at the same time, the syntactical relationship between them also. It can be deduced that the words in a sentence directly convey the sentence-meaning.

This view of comprehending a sentence is so close to the psychological analysis rather than the linguistic analysis in nature. Hence the psychological factors behind the language act can be analysed through this theory. The followers of this theory emphasize on the natural method of language analysis by which the children learn the meaning of words. They observe the speech act of elders and their activity following the utterance, and they come to know the significance of the words. When a person says to another "bring the cow", the latter brings the cow accordingly. A child, who hears the sentence uttered by the former and observes the action that follows, understands that the sentence "bring the cow" signifies an action of bringing the cow. Later, the speaker again says "bring the horse" and the latter brings a horse. Observing this, the child again infers that the sentence "bring the horse" signifies the action of bringing horse. By comparing these two sentences, he understands that the word "bring" is common in the two sentences and it must denote the command to bring and the two different words "cow" and "horse" must refer to the two different animals. Thus, by the mental process of exclusion and inclusion (*āvāpa* and *udvāpa*), the child develops a general idea of the meaning of the individual words. Later, the child is able to understand the meaning of even a new sentence containing the words he has already come across. This is well explained in the Śabdakhaṇḍa of *Siddhāntamuktāvalī*.

> *evam vyavahārādapi yathā prayojakavṛddhena ghaṭamānayetyuktaṁ tacchrutvā prayojyavṛddhena ghaṭa ānītastadavadhārya pārśvastho bālo ghaṭānayanarūpakāryaṁ ghaṭamānayeti śabdaprayojyamityavadhārayati* ।
> *tataśca ghaṭaṁ naya gāṁ bādhānetyādivākyād āvāpodvāpābhyaṁ ghaṭādipadānāṁ kāryānvitaghaṭādau śaktiṁ gṛhṇāti ... prathamataḥ kāryānvitaghaṭādau śaktyavadhāraṇe 'pi lāghavena paścāttasya parityāgaucityāt* ॥
>
> – As part of *Kārikāvalī* 1988: 561-63

Kunjunni Raja (1963: 199) opines that "the *anvitābhidhāna* view is accepted by the ancient Mīmāṁsakas Jaimini and Śabara". The passage from the *Śābarabhāṣya*, which was argued by the Abhihitānvayavādins to support their view, is criticized as fallacious by the followers of this school (under Jaimini I.1.25). They explain the same passage as supporting their view. According to this, words convey their meaning as qualified by one another. Abhinavagupta refers to this theory in his *Locana* as Dīrghavyāpāravāda. This is because in this theory, there is no limit to the extent of meaning that an expression can convey (quoted in Raja 1963: 199).

These two theories of verbal cognition propounded by the Sakhaṇḍa school differ in many perspectives. The followers of these theories raise objection against each other. But modern scholars have tried to reconcile the two theories. Mukula Bhaṭṭa says that both these theories contain partial truth. When the comprehension of a sentence is analysed from the point of view of the words, the *abhihitānvaya* theory seems to be preferable. But when it is viewed from the point of view of the sentence, the *anvitābhidhāna* theory must be given the preference (Raja 1963: 212). Bhartṛhari analyses these two theories when he discusses the definitions of a sentence. He concludes that both the theories reveal only partial truth and thus a sentence is an indivisible *sphoṭa* and sentence-meaning is *pratibhā*, the undivided semantic unit flashes in the mind.

NAIYĀYIKAS' VIEW ON SENTENCE-MEANING

Nyāyaśāstra is renowned as Pramāṇaśāstra, and hence, the concepts of sentence and sentence-meaning are not the only concern of it. As Jayanta Bhaṭṭa states, the ancient Naiyāyikas did not give much importance to the discussions on language (*Nyāyamañjarī* 1970: 143). But it is to be noted that the school of Navya-Nyāya took the matter seriously and made remarkable contribution in the study of language. For them, sentence is the collection of words and sentence-meaning is the collection of word-meanings. *Śābdabodha* is the term they use to represent the cognition of the meaning of a sentence. It is already discussed that Naiyāyikas also admit the theory of *abhihitānvaya*, with a slight difference from that of the Bhāṭṭa school of Mīmāṁsā, to explain the process of verbal cognition. Thus, the mutual connection between the word-meanings (*saṁsarga*) is the sentence-meaning. Viśvanātha expounds the complete process of verbal cognition in a single verse:

> *padajñānantu karaṇaṁ dvāraṁ tatra padārthadhīḥ* ।
> *śābdabodhaḥ phalaṁ tatra śaktidhīḥ sahakāriṇī* ॥
> – *Kārikāvalī* 1988: 546

Laugākṣī Bhāskara states that the meaning of a sentence consists in the mutual relation of the meanings expressed by the words:

> *padopasthitānāṁ mithaḥ saṁsargaḥ vākyārthaḥ* ।
> – *Tarkakaumudī* 1886: 44

According to Jagadīśa, sentence-meaning is the mutual relation of word-meanings, and in this relation, one meaning is correlated with another (*Śabdaśaktiprakāśikā* 2002: 22). Thus, it is obvious that almost all scholars of the Nyāya school accept the mutual relation of word-meanings as the sentence-meaning. It must be noted that, according to this philosophy, sentence-meaning is not to be taken as the primary or secondary meanings of a sentence. It is because this school does not accept either the primary significatory power (*śakti*) or the secondary one (*lakṣaṇā*) in a sentence. To the Naiyāyikas, word is the meaningful unit of language and it expresses its primary meaning through *śakti*. *Śakti* is the will of God, which determines the meaning of the word:

> *asmāt padādayamartho boddhavya itīśvarecchā śaktiḥ* ।
> – *Tarkasaṁgraha* 1971: 151

Navya-Naiyāyikas describe *śakti* as the will of the speaker, which assigns the meaning to the word.

Though the ancient works of the Nyāya school did not emphasize on the discussions about language studies, later texts like the *Śabdaśaktiprakāśikā*, *Vyutpattivāda* and *Nyāyamañjarī* gave special stress on Naiyāyika's view about the complex phenomenon of verbal cognition. In the Nyāya tradition, Jayanta, the author of *Nyāyamañjarī*, was the first, who elaborately discussed the concept of sentence-meaning. In this work, he discusses the theories of verbal comprehension in detail. He refers to diverse views held by the preceptors (*tatra vipratipattiśca bahurūpā vipaścitām* – *Nyāyamañjarī* 1970: 300), and rejects all these views. Besides, he also refutes the grammarians' theory of *pratibhā*, Anvitābhidhānavāda and Abhihitānvayavāda (ibid.: 335). After rejecting all these views, Jayanta introduces a unique idea about the cognition of sentence-meaning, known as Tātparyavāda. According to him, the word *tātparya* signifies the power of word which conveys the related meaning of the words in a sentence. Thus Jayanta states that *tātparya* is the cause of the cognition of sentence-meaning. In Navya-Nyāya, this power of words is called *saṁsarga-maryādā*. In the school of Navya-Nyāya, this term refers to the syntactic expectancy of words (*ākāṅkṣā*). Gadādhara Bhaṭṭa remarks that the meaning of a sentence, which is the relation that exists among the individual meanings of the words, is put forth by the *saṁsarga-maryādā* (syntactic expectancy):

> *ekapadārthe 'parapadārthasya saṁsargaḥ saṁsarga-maryādayā bhāsate* । – *Vyutpattivāda* 1973: 1

Thus Naiyāyikas reject all the different views regarding the verbal comprehension of a sentence presented by the other systems such as Grammar and Mīmāṁsā. They maintain that the verb in a sentence is not important, but the nominative substantive (*prathamāntārtha*) is the primary substantive (*mukhya-viśeṣya*) in the sentence. All the remaining parts in a sentence are the qualifiers of that word.[1]

SENTENCE-MEANING IN OTHER SYSTEMS OF KNOWLEDGE

In the school of Grammar, ancient preceptors like Pāṇini, Kātyāyana and Patañjali have not explicitly discussed on the nature of sentence-meaning. Still, some remarkable observations can be found in their works. Pāṇini comprehended all his ideas on the concept of sentence in the aphorism *samarthaḥ padavidhiḥ* (II.1.1). While commenting upon the aphorism *prātipadikārthaliṅgaparimāṇavacanamātre prathamā* (Pāṇini II.3.46), Patañjali observes that adjectival–substantive relation is something different from the word-meanings and it is the sentence-meaning (*Mahābhāṣya*, under Pāṇini II.3.46). Kaiyaṭa states that sentence is *mukhya-śabda* (prime word) and the sentence-meaning is the *mukhya-śabdārtha* (prime meaning). This view of sentence-meaning is in the nature of the relation among

[1] This view of Naiyāyikas is explained under Subsection "Theory of Prathamāntārthamukhyaviśeṣyakaśābdabodha" on p. 57.

the word-meanings (under Pāṇini I.2.45). While commenting upon this statement, Nāgeśa points out that there is a relation between a sentence and its meaning, known as *śakti* (Udyota, under Pāṇini I.2.45).

An ancient grammarian Vyāḍi also presented some unique views on the nature of sentence-meaning. He held that the meaning of a word is any particular of a class (*dravya*). According to him, the function of a word in a sentence is to distinguish the thing it signifies from all the similar things. Thus, the meaning of a sentence cannot be taken as the mutual connection of the word-meanings, but the mutual exclusion of those meanings. The early stages of the *apoha* doctrine maintained by the Buddhists can be traced in these views of Vyāḍi (Raja 1963: 193).

The Buddhist tradition made remarkable contributions to the semantic analysis of words and sentences. The idea of the Buddhist logicians about the essence of meaning is known as Apohavāda (the theory of *apoha*). They maintain that the essence of meaning is characterized by negation and that words have no direct reference to objective realities. Diṅnāga, the famous Buddhist logician, states that words deal directly with *vikalpas*, which are the conceptual images constructed in the mind. Therefore, the relation between the words and the external object is not real. The conceptual image, denoted by a word is characterized by the negation of all its counter-correlates or *anyāpoha*.

vikalpayonayaḥ śabdāḥ vikalpāḥ śabdayonayaḥ ।

– Diṅnāga, quoted in Raja 1963: 78 fn

This is the core of the theory of *apoha*, developed by the Buddhists.

This concept of negative approach to the meaning is also admitted in the case of compounds and sentences by the Buddhists. In the compound word "blue lotus", the term blue excludes all lotuses that are not blue and the term lotus excludes all the blue things that are not lotuses. Thus the expression signifies the exclusion of non-blue and non-lotus. A sentence-meaning is also imported in the same way. Though the meanings of the individual words are treated as negative, the import of a sentence is taken as positive in nature. This theory of negative approach towards meaning has been criticized by the Mīmāṁsakas and Naiyāyikas. But in recent times, similar concepts about meaning have been developed by modern linguists like Ferdinand de Saussure (Raja 1963: 85).

Three Views on the Semantic Interpretation of Sentence

The semantic interpretation of a sentence is called verbal cognition or verbal import, through which, the relation among the meanings of the words in a sentence is comprehended. Among the meanings of individual words in a sentence, one is manifested as *mukhya-viśeṣya* (primary substantive). Different systems hold different views regarding the primary substantive in a sentence. Generally, there are three views on the semantic interpretation of a sentence. These three views differ from one another regarding the primary substantive in the sentence. These views are discussed here in a nutshell.

THEORY OF VYĀPĀRĀRTHAMUKHYAVIŚEṢYAKAŚĀBDABODHA

Grammarians generally accept *vyāpāra* (activity), which is the meaning of the verbal root as the primary substantive. According to them, when the desired activity is performed, the goal is realized. Thus in a sentence, the root-meaning is the primary substantive and the meanings of remaining parts are treated as qualifiers. They refer to the statement in the *Nirukta*, *bhāvapradhānamākhyātam* (4), in which, the word *bhāva* denotes the root-meaning and the root simultaneously denotes *vyāpāra* (activity) and *phala* (result):

> *phalavyāpārayordhāturāśraye tu tiṅaḥ smṛtāḥ* ।
> – *Vaiyākaraṇabhūṣṇasāra* 1

Among them, *vyāpāra* is primarily qualified (*viśeṣya*) in a sentence, while the other meaning *phala* is only attributive (*viśeṣaṇa*) to the former. The suffix in the verb denotes *kāla* (substratum factor) and *āśraya* (number factor) and these two are (*viśeṣaṇa*) to the action (*kriyā*). Thus, the sentence, *caitraḥ grāmaṁ gacchati* (*caitra* goes to the village), gives rise to the cognition in the form:

> *caitrābhinnaikakartṛkaḥ grāmaniṣṭhasaṁyogānukūlaḥ vartamānakālikaḥ vyāpāraḥ* ।

Even if the sentence is in passive voice, the cognition is the same.

THEORY OF PRATHAMĀNTĀRTHAMUKHYAVIŚEṢYAKAŚĀBDABODHA

Naiyāyikas uphold that the primary substantive (*mukhya-viśeṣya*) of the sentence is the meaning of the noun in the nominative case. The meanings of the remaining parts are only qualifiers. According to them, the cognition that arises from the sentence, *caitraḥ grāmaṁ gacchati*, is as:

> *grāmaniṣṭhasaṁyogānukūlavyāpārānukūlakṛtyāśrayaḥ caitraḥ* ।

THEORY OF AKHYĀTĀRTHAMUKHYAVIŚEṢYAKAŚĀBDABODHA

According to the Mīmāṁsakas, *bhāvanā* (idea of action), which is the meaning of *ākhyāta* (verbal suffix) is the primary substantive (*mukhya-viśeṣya*) of the sentence. Yāska states: *bhāvapradhānamākhyātam* (*Nirukta* 2002: 4). Mīmāṁsakas explain the statement as the word *bhāva* has reference only to the action or *bhāvanā* and not to the root-meaning as argued by the grammarians. Thus, the sentence "*caitra* goes to the village" can be explained as:

> *caitraniṣṭhagrāmasaṁyogānukūlavyāpārānukūlā kṛtiḥ* ।

Apart from these three views, some scholars put forth their own perspectives regarding the primary substantive in the sentence.

Jayanta Bhaṭṭa describes that *phala* (the result), the meaning of the verbal root is the primary substantive (*mukhya-viśeṣya*). The school of Viśiṣṭādvaita upholds that, the meaning of the verbal suffix is the agent (*kartā*) and is the primary substantive (*mukhya-viśeṣya*) in the verbal cognition (Tatacharya 2005: 43).

Requisites for Understanding the Sentence-Meaning

It is already discussed that *śābdabodha* is the term used by Indian linguists to map the process of cognition of sentence-meaning. In the Sakhaṇḍa school, the sentence is an aggregate of its parts which are syntactically connected (*sākāṅkṣā*). The knowledge of this syntactic unity of sentence is mainly due to *ākāṅkṣā* (mutual expectancy of words), *yogyatā* (congruity or consistency of the meaning) and *āsatti* or *sannidhi* (proximity) of words. These three inevitable conditions for the understanding of sentence-meaning were first introduced by the Mīmāṁsakas.

> *ākāṅkṣā sannidhānam ca yogyatā ceti ca trayam* ।
> *saṁbandhakāraṇatvena kḷptaṁ nānantaraśrutiḥ* ॥
> – *Tantravārtika* 1929: 455

Later, these concepts were taken up by almost all the other systems of knowledge in the Sakhaṇḍa school of sentence, with slight changes. In addition to these three, a fourth condition, known as *tātparya-jñāna*, was also introduced. It is the intention of the speaker or the general purport of the sentence.

ĀKĀṄKṢĀ (SYNTACTIC EXPECTANCY)

The word *ākāṅkṣā* is derived from the root *kāṅkṣ* which signifies "to desire". Thus, the term literally means the desire to know something. Vācaspati Miśra defines *ākāṅkṣā* as the desire to know on the part of the listener (Tatacharya 2005: 44). It can be simply defined as the desire on the part of the listeners to know other words or their meaning to complete the sense. A word is said to have mutual expectancy for another, only if it cannot, without the latter, produce knowledge of its interconnection in an utterance (Raja 1963: 156). In a sentence, a word (noun or verb) always requires another word to complete the meaning of the sentence. If one says *gāmānaya* (bring the cow), the verb "bring" requires a noun in the nominative case to complete the sentence-meaning. At the same time, a series of words such as "cow, horse, man, elephant" does not convey a unified sense, as there is no connection between them because of the absence of *ākāṅkṣā*.

Ākāṅkṣā can be of two types, viz. *utthitākāṅkṣā* and *utthāpyākāṅkṣā*. The former is the actual expectancy of one word for the other to give a unified sense. The latter is the potential expectancy which could be awakened if necessary. For example, when one says to another "bring the cow", the latter may ask the question "which colour"? Then the speaker has to imply an adjective like "white" and "black". These potential expectancies have no limit because it can be awakened when the listener necessitates (Chatterjee 1939: 367). While expounding this concept, Raja refers to two types of *ākāṅkṣā*, described by the Naiyāyikas; one is psychological and the other is syntactical or grammatical (1963: 163). The grammatical expectancy between the words in a sentence necessitates the syntactic completeness of the sentence, while the psychological expectancy gives rise to the semantic unity of the sentence. It is well explained by Nāgeśa, the great grammarian, as: *ākāṅkṣā* is the desire on the part of the listeners on hearing a word in a sentence to know the idea, which can be related to its meaning in order to get a complete sense (*Paramalaghumañjūṣā* 1985: 33). Here, the expectancy is on the part of listeners and is superimposed on words and their meanings.

YOGYATĀ (CONGRUITY)

Yogyatā is defined as the logical compatibility of the words in a sentence for the mutual association (*arthābādho yogyatā* –

Tarkasaṁgraha 1971: 154). The sense or nonsense of a sentence depends upon this concept. Śālikanātha gives a vivid explanation on the nature of *yogyatā* in his *Vākyārthamātṛkāvṛtti*. He states that the capability of words in a sentence for mutual association and this competence is to be known from experience (quoted in Raja 1963: 164). Almost all the philosophers explain this by illustrating the sentence *agninā siñcati* (he drenches with fire). When one says "he drenches with water", there is *yogyatā* (consistency of the meaning), since drenching is normally done with a liquid substance like water. Thus, the sense of drenching and that of water have no incompatibility. But in the sentence "he drenches with fire", the idea of drenching is not compatible with that of fire. Thus, we cannot say there is *yogyatā*.

There are combinations which are inconceivable and conceivable in the world. "A circular square" is a combination that cannot be conceived in any way. The ideas like "the rabbit's horn" or "the son of an infertile woman" can be conceived anyway, but are against the experience. The latter example may be incompatible with reality, but it does not prevent the verbal comprehension. Bhartṛhari and Kumārila are in favour of this view (*Vākyapadīya* I.155 and *Ślokavārtika* 46). Sometimes the lack of *yogyatā* points to the metaphorical meaning of a word in the sentence. According to some scholars the apparent incompatibility of the expressed sense is an essential condition for *lakṣaṇā* (Raja 1963: 166).

SANNIDHI (PROXIMITY)

Sannidhi or *āsatti* is generally defined as the condition that the utterance of the words in a sentence should be contiguous in time:

> *padānām avilambenocchāraṇaṁ sannidhiḥ* ।
>
> – *Tarkasaṁgraha* 1971: 154

In other words, this is the uninterrupted utterance of words that they are in juxtaposition. When a person utters words at long intervals of time, they cannot establish any interrelation among them. What is worthy of note here is that the mere immediate sequence of utterance does not give rise to *sannidhi.* Kumārila Bhaṭṭa calls this immediate sequence of utterance as *anantara-śruti.* He distinguishes *sannidhi* from *anantara-śruti* as the continuous apprehension of words or their meaning in the mind (*Tantravārtika* 1929: 455). Prabhākara describes this concept in a different perspective. He believes that *sannidhi* is only the contiguity of cognition of the sense and not necessarily of words actually uttered (Raja 1963: 167). According to the Navya-Nyāya school, even if the words are separated, there is *sannidhi* as in the case of a verse. They hold that the meanings of the words are recollected without any interruption through their expressive power. This recollection is termed as *samūhālaṁbana-smṛti* (collective cognition).

TĀTPARYA (IMPORT)

Apart from the three auxiliary causes of knowing the sentence-meaning described, some Indian schools of thought like Nyāya and Vedānta accept the knowledge of the intention of speaker as the fourth cause. Generally, it can be defined as being uttered with the desire of producing a certain meaning. It is to be noted that different philosophers maintain different views in accepting *tātparya* (speaker's intention) as the cause of comprehending the sentence-meaning. This difference is due to their views as to the nature of the knowledge derived from language. Naiyāyikas give great importance to the speaker's intention in fixing the meaning of an utterance. The reason is that they accept *śabda* as one of the means of valid knowledge, only when it is uttered by a trustworthy person. Thus, the intention of the trustworthy person is important for them. According to them, in Vedic sentences as well as in ordinary sentences, it is the intention that precedes the cognition of meaning. In the case of Vedic sentences, they assume the intention of God (even in the case of the parrot imitating the utterance of people, Naiyāyikas assume the intention of God):

> *śukavākye bhagavadicchaiva gatiḥ* । – *Nyāyakośa* 1978: 326

It is again mentioned that, in ordinary sentences, the meaning is associated with the word by intention. The word *ghaṭa* in the sentence *ghaṭamānaya* signifies pot by the intention of the speaker.

> *pare tu ghaṭādiśabdasthale 'pi ghaṭapadam kumbhaparam lakṣaṇayā paṭaparam veti saṁśaye ghaṭaśābdabodhābhāvāt sarvatra tātparyaniścayaḥ kāraṇamityāhuḥ* ।
> – *Nyāyakośa* 1978: 327

If this extreme view is accepted, the normal signification of words would always depend on the intention of the speaker, which makes the linguistic communication impossible.

Thus, Vedāntins and Mīmāṁsakas reject this view of Naiyāyikas. They maintain that every word has an inherent capacity to express its meaning. Similarly, a sentence is also capable of expressing a unified sense in the form of the mutual association of the word-meanings. Generally, Mīmāṁsakas believe in the theory of *apauruṣeya*, in which, the verbal comprehension has no reference to the speaker at all. They also maintain that the interconnection between word and meaning is inherent. Hence a sentence, though unintelligible to the speaker, has an inherent capacity to convey its meaning. Though the Vedāntins are against the views of Naiyāyikas, they admit, however, the role of speaker's intention in knowing the sentence-meaning. According to them, the speaker's intention has a vital role in comprehending the meaning of ambiguous sentences. Thus, it can be assumed that, by the term *tātparya*, Naiyāyikas refer to the meaning intended by the speaker. While Mīmāṁsakas and Vedāntins use the term to denote the meaning conveyed by the capacity of the words themselves.

It can be concluded that almost all schools of Indian thought have recognized the importance of knowing the speaker's intention in understanding the speech. Speech is mainly purposive in nature and can do its function only if the listener understands the intention of the speaker. At the same time, language is accepted as an objective instrument of communication and, thus, it must be independent of personal inclinations of the speaker.

3

The Concept of Sentence and Sentence-Meaning

Gleanings from Vākyapadīya

Language Analysis in Vākyapadīya

As discussed, Bhartṛhari presents a unique and complete analysis of the concept of language in the *Vākyapadīya*. He analyses language in three levels, viz. absolute level, communicative level and analytic level.

ABSOLUTE LEVEL

Bhartṛhari explains the absolute level of language in terms of the concept of *śabda-brahman*. This is the ultimate level of existence of language, which is beyond shape, time, qualities, etc. At this level, word is a representative of the ultimate truth. This perspective of language-essence is described in the opening verse of the *Vākyapadīya*.

> *anādinidhanam brahma śabdatattvaṁ yadakṣaram* ।
> *vivartate 'rthabhāvena prakriyā jagato yataḥ* । – 1.1

Here, it is described as the essence of the world, which is beyond the time–space limitations. Here, Bhartṛhari uses the word *śabda* with deeper significance. Thus, *śabda*, which is sequenceless in nature, underlies the sequential language.

COMMUNICATIVE LEVEL

This is the state of language when used as the speech act. Language is generally considered as the tool of communicating ideas. Ideas or thoughts are communicated in a language act. Thoughts are never bits and pieces, but appear as whole. So ideas and thoughts are also to be communicated as wholes. Thus, in communication, there must be a minimum possible unit of language. Bhartṛhari argues that the unit of language is sentence, which conveys the complete thought or idea of the speaker.[1]

ANALYTIC LEVEL

Though Bhartṛhari accepts the sentence as the unit of language, he mentions that language can be analysed into its various parts, for the purpose of studying grammar. In the third canto of *Vākyapadīya*, he explains each and every part and piece of language with their minute significances. Study of language at this level is an ideal tool to teach and learn language. The grammar level teaching and learning are significant at this analytic level of language.

Thus, it can be deduced that Bhartṛhari has a unique and complete vision on the concept of language and the speech act. The whole language theory of Bhartṛhari is erected on the concept of sentence-holism, which is emphatically described in the second canto of *Vākyapadīya*.

---

1 This can be compared to the concept of gestalt, which is used in modern psychology. Gestalt is a term, which signifies a "unified whole". Gestalt theories refer to theories of visual perception developed by German psychologists in 1920s. These theories put forth an idea that in our visual perception, we organize visual elements into groups or unified wholes. Psychologists define gestalten as a configuration or organized field that cannot be derived from the summation of its components, rather it is a unified whole.

After the three sages Pāṇini, Kātyāyana and Patañjali, it was Bhartṛhari, the great grammarian and philosopher, who discovered the depth and breadth of Sanskrit grammar. Aklujkar rightly observes that the *Vākyapadīya* is chronologically the fourth surviving work in the Pāṇinian grammatical tradition (Coward and Raja 2008: 125). As stated, Bhartṛhari examines language in three levels. In the first canto, it is conceived as *śabda-brahman*, which is the ultimate inner level of language. He also perceives language in the level of communication, which is discussed in the second canto. The entire second canto of *Vākyapadīya* is dedicated to discuss the basic unit of communication, sentence. There are different opinions as to whether word is expressive or sentence. Bhartṛhari opines that individual words and individual word-meaning are not real when compared to sentence. An idea can be expressed only by a sentence; neither by words nor by syllables and, thus, sentence is considered as the basic unit of language.

Definition of Sentence

Bhartṛhari interprets the concept of sentence in a two-dimensional way. On one side, he gives a working definition of sentence as the group of syntactically connected words, while on the other side, the term *vākya* as a synonym of *śabda*. Bhartṛhari begins his discussion on sentence by presenting available theories and definitions of sentence from various schools of thoughts. In the first two verses of the Vākyakāṇḍa, he enumerates eight different views about sentence held by the ancient thinkers.

ākhyātaśabdaḥ saṁghāto jātiḥ saṁghātavartinī ।
eko 'navayavaḥ śabdaḥ kramo budhyanusamhṛtiḥ ॥
padamādyaṁ pṛthak sarvaṁ padaṁ sākāṅkṣāmityapi ।
vākyaṁ prati matirbhinnā bahudhā nyāyavādinām ॥

– *Vākyapadīya* II.1-2

According to various views, sentence may be defined as:

1. the verb,
2. the collection of words,
3. the universal inhering in the collection of words,
4. the one indivisible word,
5. the sequence of words,
6. the unification in the mind,
7. the first word, and
8. each word requiring the others (*Vākyapadīya* II.1-2, tr. K.A.S. Iyer 1983).

These definitions may not describe all the aspects of sentence, but they can be taken as different ways of looking at sentence by different thinkers.

SAṀGHĀTAḤ VĀKYAM

The word *saṁghāta* literally means "a collection of something". In the present context, *saṁghāta* can be taken as a group of words, the meanings of which are interconnected. Thus, according to this view, sentence is the *saṁghāta* (group of words). This view can be traced in the aphorism, *samarthaḥ padavidhiḥ* of Pāṇini (II.1.1), which says that the *vidhi* related with the words depends on *sāmarthya* or the capability. While commenting this aphorism, Patañjali remarks that words are equally capable of forming sentences and compounds.[2] Bhartṛhari sets forth his view on this definition in the following verses:

kevalena padenārtho yāvānevābhidhīyate ।
vākyasthaṁ tāvato'rthasya tadāhurabhidhāyakam ॥
sambandhe sati yattvanyadādhikyam upajāyate ।
vākyarthameva taṁ prāhuranekapadasaṁśrayam ॥
– *Vākyapadīya* II.41-42

[2] The interpretation of Patañjali has already been elaborately discussed in subsection "Sentence According to the School of Vyākaraṇa" on p. 40.

Iyer translates these verses as:

> It has been declared that a word, as part of a sentence, expresses the same extent of meaning as it does when it is in isolation. Whatever extra meaning is understood when the words (in a sentence) are connected together, is the meaning of the sentence and it rests on many words.

A word, which expresses its meaning when it is in isolation, expresses the same individual meaning in the sentence also. But in a sentence, it is connected syntactically as well as semantically with the other words in the sentence and thus we understand the meaning of the sentence as a whole. Here, it should be noted that, when we understand the complete meaning of a sentence, it is different from the aggregation of individual word-meanings. Therefore, Bhartṛhari calls it as *ādhikya* in the above verse. According to this view, just as the cooking can be done with many instruments and as a vehicle travels with the help of its parts, interconnected words together denote the meaning of a sentence. Patañjali also says what we get from a sentence as "extra" can be treated as its meaning (*yadatrādhikyam vākyārthaḥ saḥ* । – *Mahābhāṣya*, under Pāṇini II.3.50).

KRAMAḤ VĀKYAM

This view is well explained by Bimal Krishna Matilal as the sentence is nothing but the "sequence" of words and the sentence-meaning belongs to this sequence (1992: 95). The followers of this school argue that there is no separate entity called sentence, but the mere sequence of the words is expressive. Bhartṛhari gives a clear picture of this definition in this verse:

> *santa eva viśeṣā ye padārtheṣu vyavasthitaḥ* ।
> *te kramād anugamyante na vākyam abhidhāyakam* ॥
> – *Vākyapadīya* 2.49

The particularizations which exist already in the word-meanings are understood from their sequence and there is no expressive sentence beyond that (*Vākyapadīya* II.49, Iyer). In fact, a sentence refers to the proper placement of words. Since this is not possible without accepting a definite order, *krama* (sequence) of words is to be accepted as a sentence. What is worthy of note here is that the sequence is a property of time.

But how can the sequence of words alone be expressive? A word also is nothing other than the sequence of phonemes and audibility is also common for phoneme and word. Then why cannot we say that sequence of phonemes is also expressive? Bhartṛhari criticizes this view upon this point. He says:

padākhyā vākyasaṁjñā ca śabdatvaṁ neṣyate tayoḥ ।
– *Vākyapadīya* II.52

While commenting on this verse, Iyer clarifies:

> The phoneme and the word are audible but mere audibility does not entitle them to be called *śabda*. For that, they must convey the meaning, they must be *vācaka*. They are not. Only sequence is so.

Both phonemes and words are audible entities and hence both of them can be treated as *śabda*. But sequence of phonemes cannot express the sentence-meaning. It is understood only from the sequence of words. Thus, sequence is the sentence and sentence-meaning is understood by the interconnection of word-meanings. Puṇyarāja also supports this view in his commentary on Vākyakāṇḍa:

tat kramaścaiva vākyam, saṁsargo vākyārtha iti ।
– *Vākyapadīya* II.53

ĀKHYĀTAŚABDAḤ VĀKYAM

The word *ākhyāta* literally means *kriyā* (verb). Yāska also states *bhāvapradhānam ākhyātam* (*Nirukta* 2002: 4), which can be translated as: *ākhyāta* is that word, in which *kriyā* has prime significance. The word *bhāva* signifies *kriyā*. Bhaṭṭojī Dīkṣita supports this view, saying:

> *vyāpāro bhāvanā saivotpādanā saiva ca kriyā* ।
> – *Vaiyākaradṇbūṣaṇasāra* 1.5

The words *vyāpāra*, *bhāvanā*, *utpādanā* and *kriyā* are used synonymously. Hence the above definition says that a sentence must have a finite verb or in several contexts, the finite verb is the sentence. The verb is considered to be the prime factor in a sentence as all the other words in the sentence are connected to the verb to give a unified sense. Because of this prime position of the verb in a sentence, Bhartṛhari puts forth the view that *ākhyāta-śabda* or the verb can be called a sentence. He explains this in the verse:

> *vākyaṁ tadapi manyante yat padaṁ caritakriyam* ।
> *antareṇa kriyāśabdaṁ vākyādeva hi darśanāt* ॥
> – *Vākyapadīya* II.325

This verse gives a vivid picture about the word *ākhyāta-śabda*. He says that even a noun impregnated with the idea of action can be treated as a sentence. According to Bhartṛhari, the word *ākhyāta* signifies not verb, but the idea of an action. Hence an idea of action should be present in a sentence. This is evidently known from the verse:

> *yāvat sidham asidhaṁ vā sādhyatvenābhidhīyate* ।
> *āśritakramarūpatvāt sā kriyetyabhidhīyate* ॥
> – *Vākyapadīya* III.8.1

Bhartṛhari describes verb as a group of actions performed in a sequential manner. No matter it is *siddha* or *asiddha* or *sādhya* and hence a verb (*kriyā*) is that word, which signifies an action.

By defining sentence as *ākhyātaṁ sāvyayakārakaviśeṣaṇaṁ vākyam* (Kātyāyana, under Pāṇini II.1.1), Kātyāyana also seems to be in favour of this view. He opines that a verb qualified by *avyaya*, *kāraka* and *viśeṣaṇa* can be called a sentence. Sometimes even in the absence of these qualifiers, a single verb also can be a sentence. In the absence of qualifiers, they can be supplied naturally through a device called *adhyāhāra*. In most of the cases, a sentence will not be complete without a verb.

PADAMĀDYAṀ VĀKYAM

Those who hold the view that the first word is sentence opine that a word in an expression or sentence is not a separate entity but it is syntactically connected with other words in the sentence or it is *sākāṅkṣam*. Hence words in a sentence do not convey their individual meaning, but a connected meaning which arises from their mutual connection. Each word expresses a meaning in connection with another word which can be called a connected meaning. Bhartṛhari explains this view as:

> *viśeṣaśabāḥ keṣāñcit sāmānyapratirūpakaḥ* ।
> *śabdāntarābhisambandhād vyajyante pratipattṛṣu* ॥
> – *Vākyapadīya* II.17

A word does not convey its individual meaning in the sentence, though it seems to be the same as in another expression. It conveys a meaning as connected with the other words in the expression. So the meaning of the sentence is already contained in, though only vaguely, the first word. Thus the first word in a sentence can also be treated as a sentence.

An objection may be raised here that, if the very first word itself denotes the meaning of the sentence, the remaining words would be useless. Bhartṛhari answers this saying that the remaining words in the sentence make the sentence-meaning expressed by the first word clearer. Hearers understand the meaning better when all the words are uttered. This is explained in the verse:

teṣāṁ tu kṛtsno vākyārthaḥ pratibhedaṁ samāpyate ।
vyaktopavyañjanā sidhirarthasya pratipattṛśu ॥
– *Vākyapadīya* II.18

This verse states that the whole of the sentence meaning is contained in each word and hearers understand the meaning better when all the words in the sentence are uttered (*Vākyapadīya* II.18, tr. Iyer). Hence we can say that the meaning of a sentence is the meaning of its first word as connected with the meanings of other words (*sākāṅkṣam*). Here, the *Vṛtti* says that the very first word expresses its meaning as connected with the meanings of the other words and hence the remaining words denote no new meaning apart from the connected meaning of the first word. But they only make the meaning of the sentence clearer which is already expressed obscurely by the first word. Thus from the hearer's point of view, the sentence-meaning is clear only when all the words are uttered. The followers of this view state that no word conveys a meaning which is not connected with the meanings of the other.

PṚTHAK SARVAṀ PADAṀ SĀKĀṄKṢAṀ VĀKYAM

This definition of sentence is only a modified view of the above, which says that each word in the sentence contains the whole sentence-meaning and hence each word can be called a sentence. Bhartṛhari puts forth this view in the same verse, which is cited above (*Vākyapadīya* II.18). Those who hold this view says that the whole sentence-meaning is concentrated not only in the first word, but in each word in a sentence.

EKO 'NAVAYAVAḤ ŚABDAḤ VĀKYAM

Bhartṛhari introduces this view saying that a sentence is not formed by the mere aggregation of words. A sentence is an indivisible unit of language. It is for the sake of convenience as well as for facilitating our learning and understanding of a language that we split the indivisible sentence into smaller parts called words and phonemes.[3] Hence, even though a sentence appears to have sequence, it is really without any. This indivisible sentence is either internal or external to the language user.[4] When it exists within the speaker before utterance, it is internal and as it is manifested through speech process, it is external also (*Vākyapadīya* II.19). This indivisible unit, which is expressive of meaning, might be understood as the indivisible *sphoṭa*. Here, Bhartr̥hari elaborately expounds his views of sentence *sphoṭa*.

According to this view, sentence is the indivisible external *sphoṭa*, which is eternal. To explain this unique concept, he describes an example of *citra-jñāna* (cognition of a multicoloured picture). In Bhartr̥hari's words:

> *citrasyaikasvarūpasya yathā bhedanidarśanaiḥ* ।
> *nīlādibhiḥ samākhyānam kriyate bhinnalakṣaṇaiḥ* ॥
> – *Vākyapadīya* II.8

Just as a multicoloured picture is explained through its different colours which belong to its parts, the sentence, which is self-sufficient and complete, is explained through individual words which require one another (*Vākyapadīya* II.8-9, tr. Iyer). A picture

---

[3] Bhartr̥hari introduced a unique method for the analysis of a sentence into its parts, which is named as *apoddhāra*. This is a mental process, through which, words are differentiated from the sentence. In reality, sentence is a unified whole, but when the meaning of the sentence is cognized; the hearer differentiates the words from it afterwards.

[4] Modern scholars explain the concept of *sphoṭa* as the language symbol or as an "auditory image", which is sequenceless and underlies the uttered speech. The listener first grasps this language symbol through the uttered speech, which is sequential in nature. This is known as the external *śabda* or *sphoṭa*. Later, this language symbol (*sphoṭa*) transforms into meaning as a flash of understanding known as *pratibhā*. This intuitive level of *śabda* is the internal *sphoṭa*.

can convey a complete sense of understanding in its whole, but can be explained through the different colours in it. The same is happening in the cognition of a sentence also. A sentence is self-sufficient and self-expressive of a complete thought, but is explained through individual words. Hence, the appearance of divisibility of sentences and sentence-meanings is deceptive. Matilal mentions that this view is like the "cognition of multiplicity" (Matilal 1992: 97).

This view gets clear as we go through the commentary of Puṇyarāja on the verse 2.7. It says:

> Bhartr̥hari really wants to set forth the following view; the sentence is the *sphoṭa* either external or internal. It is external when it is clearly uttered. Till then, it is internal. In any case, it is indivisible. It has two aspects: the sound aspect and the meaning aspect, which are identified with one another. It is essentially in the nature of knowledge or consciousness because it illuminates an object. Because of articulation, it assumes the form of sound. Though indivisible, it appears to have divisions just as our complex cognition, though one, it appears to have inner differentiation because of the objects in it. The picture is one, but we seem to see different colours within it. That is what happens with the sentence and the sentence-meaning. Both are indivisible like the flavour of a cold drink, or the juice in a pea-hen's egg, or the form of a picture, the *narasiṁha*, the *gavaya* and our perception of a picture. The indivisible sentence is *sphoṭa* and the indivisible sentence-meaning is *pratibhā*. But both appear to have divisions. – *Vākyapadīya* II.7, tr. Iyer

Grammarians accept this view as the *akhaṇḍa-vākyasphoṭa* theory. They accept *sphoṭa*, which is manifested through uttered sounds and is indivisible. According to them, words and syllables are only imaginary tools for explaining the sentence. Bhartr̥hari clearly states his view about sentence-*sphoṭa* in the first *kāṇḍa* itself:

> *pade na varṇā vidyante varṇeṣvavayavā na ca* ।
> *vākyāt padānām atyantaṁ praviveko na kaścana* ॥
> – *Vākyapadīya* I.73

What we can deduce from this verse is that the syllables in a word and words in a sentence are not real, but only conceptual. So we cannot differentiate a sentence into words. Nāgeśa also refers to this theory in his *Paramalaghumañjūṣā* as:

> *tatra prativākyaṁ saṅketagrahāsambhavād vākyānvākhyānasya laghūpāyenāśakyatvācca kalpanayā padāni pravibhajya pade prakr̥tipratyayabhāgān pravibhajya kalpitābhyāmanvayavyatirekābhyāṁ tattadarthavibhāgaṁ śāstramātraviṣayaṁ parikalpayanti smācāryāḥ* । – 1985: 6

JĀTIḤ SAṀGHĀTAVARTINĪ VĀKYAM

In this view, Bhartr̥hari states that the universal of the constitutive group of words can be assumed as a sentence. It is well described by Bhartr̥hari as:

> *yathākṣepaviśeṣe 'pi karmabhedo na gr̥hyate* ।
> *āvr̥ttau vyajyate jatiḥ karmabhirbhramaṇādibhiḥ* ॥
> – *Vākyapadīya* II.20

Bhartr̥hari explains this view by elucidating an example of rotating an object. A movement like rotating or turning consists of a series of momentary movements. While rotating an object, it starts from a point and ends at the same point and the next rotation replaces it. Each rotation is unique in their speed, etc. and hence they cannot coexist and form a whole, of which they would be parts. Hence, we may consider the universal of the movement called rotation for the cognition of the whole. There are other movements such as lifting occur during the process, but because of the resemblance between these actions and rotation, this universal is capable of producing the cognition of the whole rotation. The process is similar in the cognition of a sentence also. In an utterance, syllables, words and sentences are expressed by *dhvani*s and the listener grasps the whole meaning of the utterance. Though the listener grasps the *sphoṭa* of phonemes, words and sentences, which may differ from another, the manifesting sound appear to be the same. It is clearly stated in the *Vṛtti* of *Vākyapadīya* as:

> *śabdajātereva vākyatve bhramaṇatvādayo dṛṣṭāntatvenopanyastāḥ* । *varṇatvapadatvavākyatvāni hi tulyātulyopavyañjanāni yāvat tulyopavyañjanasannipātaḥ tāvat buddhibhedam kurvanti* । *katham? apacitadhvanivyaṅgyastāvad eko varṇaḥ, tasyābhi-vyaktinimittaiḥ sadṛśairanyaiśca śrutibhinnairekam niravayavam ca padam vyajyate thataiva tulyātulyaiḥ pracitatamairvākyamiti* ।
>
> –II.21

Puṇyarāja opines that this definition is what Bhartṛhari elaborates as *jāti-sphoṭa* while the former as *vyakti-sphoṭa.*

BUDHYANUSAMHṚTIḤ VĀKYAM

Both the above definitions refer to the external *sphoṭa*, which is described under *Vākyapadīya* II.1.7. Among the definitions explained above, the former (*eko 'navayavaḥ śabdaḥ*) regards the sentence as a particular whole while the latter views it as a universal (*jātiḥ saṁghātavartinī*). The later grammarians called them as *vyakti-sphoṭa* and *jāti-sphoṭa* respectively. This is evidently stated by Puṇyarāja as:

> *evaṁ tāvad bahīrūpaṁ vyaktisphoṭaṁ jātisphoṭaṁ vā vācakam āśritya vākyaṁ vyākhyātam* । – *Vākyapadīya* II.29

The view that sentence is *budhyanusaṁhṛti* represents the internal *sphoṭa*. In this definition, the term *budhyanusaṁhṛti* can be explained as *anukrameṇa saṁhṛtiḥ anusaṁhṛtiḥ, kalpitānām padabudhīnām anusaṁhṛtiḥ budhyanusaṁhṛtiḥ*, which means the words in a sentence are only imaginary and are dissolved or unified in the cognition. The sentence is the real word and the words are only for the purpose of analysis (*apoddhāra*). This real word is an inner entity which is one, indivisible and without any inner sequence. This inner entity cannot be separated as sentence and meaning; while it consists of consciousness. All these views are discussed by Bhartṛhari as:

yadantaḥ śabdatattvaṁ tu nādairekaṁ prakāśitam ।
tamāhurapare śabdaṁ tasya vākye tathaikatā ॥
– *Vākyapadīya* II.30

What is peculiar to this view is that the thoughts or ideas, which are communicated by uttered words, are also referred to as language by Bhartṛhari. Thus, he enunciates a psycholinguistic perspective of language in this view of sentence.

The external aspects of the word, *jāti* and *vyakti*, have already been pointed out under the definitions *jātiḥ saṅghātavartinī* and *eko 'navayavaḥ śabdaḥ* respectively. It can be seen in the *Vṛtti* that this external sentence is like the written symbols (*akṣaracihnavat*). Sometimes we mistake these symbols to the real word. It is only a symbol of the real sentence which is an inner entity and is an indivisible unit (*Vākyapadīya* II.30).

Bhartṛhari again points out that not only sentence, but the meaning of sentence is also indivisible

arthabhāgaistathā teṣām āntaro 'rthaḥ prakāśyate
– *Vākyapadīya* II.31

It says that the inner meaning or the sentence-meaning is manifested by the parts of the sentence. Word and meaning are inseparable divisions (*apṛthaksthitau*) of the one inner principle (*Vākyapadīya* II.31). Hence both sentence and its meaning are inner entities and are identical. After explaining this, Puṇyarāja puts forth a relevant question. It is well known and accepted by all the philosophers that word is "the expression" and meaning is "what is expressed". According to the verse cited above, if both the inner entities and identical, how can they said to be distinguished as expression and expressed to each other? Bhartṛhari, keeping this doubt in mind, proceeds to next verse:

> *prakāśakaprakāśyatvaṁ kāryakāraṇarūpatā* ।
> *antarmātrātmanastasya śabdatattvasya sarvadā* ॥
> – *Vākyapadīya* II.32

The inner word-principle has got both the powers of being expressive (*prakāśaka*) and of being expressed (*prakāśya*). In other words, the same word-principle can be the cause as well as the effect. In short, the "One Word-Principle" contains the seeds of all manifestations (*Vākyapadīya* II.32). This is well stated in the first *kāṇḍa* of *Vākyapadīya*:

> *ekasya sarvabījasya yasya ceyamanekadhā* ।
> *bhoktṛbhoktavyarūpeṇa bhogarūpeṇa ca sthiti* ॥
> – *Vākyapadīya* I.4

The language principle *śabda-tattva*, which acts as the cause of all utterances is one, but manifested as many, like *bhoktā*, *bhoktavya* and *bhoga*.

We may have a vivid perception of this view as we go through the *Vṛtti* of II.31, which interprets the process of hearing and understanding of an utterance. When an utterance is heard, the process of understanding is like this:

> It is well known that the word principle is mainly the indivisible inner entity and that it is grasped through its indefinable and unreal parts. Similarly, the meanings reflected in the intellect are experienced as identical with the external objects. This is according to the view that it is eternal; it manifests itself according to the power of sequence of the intellect. An external object is not fit for practical purposive usage without the intellect with which it is wrongly identified. All worldly usage is done with objects which have been grasped in the intellect. Thus both the word and the object are in the intellect.
>
> – *Vākyapadīya* II.31, tr. Iyer

It is clear from this description that ultimately the external form of word and external objects are transient as well as unreal, but at the same time they inspire the intellect. Even though intellect is without any sequence, it has the power to grasp things in a sequential manner. Hence when an external object is perceived, it inspires the intellect, where meaning and word are identical.

Sakhaṇḍa and Akhaṇḍa Schools of Sentence

Indian scholars have tried to expound the real nature of sentence and sentence-meaning by analysis, synthesis and abstraction (a method introduced by Bhartṛhari called *apoddhāra*). Whether sentence can be analysed or not, remained a debated issue from ancient times. Bhartṛhari notes that there are two schools regarding the notion of the sentence and sentence-meaning, viz. *akhaṇḍa-pakṣa* and *sakhaṇḍa-pakṣa*.[5] The controversy between these two schools is mainly regarding the primary units of meaning; whether it is sentence or word. An earlier reference can be found in the *Ṛgvedaprātiśākhya*, in which it is stated as *saṁhitā padaprakṛtiḥ* (II.1). This statement is explained in two different ways by the followers of Akhaṇḍa and Sakhaṇḍa schools of sentence to authenticate their theses. The term *saṁhitā*, in this statement, denotes "sentence" and the word *prakṛti* refers to "origin". If the compound word *padaprakṛtiḥ* is analysed as *tatpuruṣa* compound, the derivation would be like *padānāṁ prakṛtiḥ*. Then, it signifies that the sentence (*saṁhitā*) is the origin of words. Here, sentence is the unit of language and words are differentiated later, from this unit. If the statement is taken as *bahuvrīhi* compound, it can be described as *padāni prakṛtiḥ yasyāḥ sā, padaprakṛtiḥ*. This gives an idea that words are the units of meaning and sentence is nothing more than the collection of words.

---

[5] Matilal describes the former school as "sentence-holism" and the latter as "atomism" (1992: 106).

Among the definitions of sentence explained above, some definitions come under the view that sentence is the aggregation of its parts (*sakhaṇḍa-pakṣa*). *Saṁghāta* (collection of words), *krama* (sequence of words), *ākhyāta-śabda* (verb), *padamādyam* (first word) and *pr̥thak sarvaṁ padaṁ sākāṅkṣam* (each word requiring others) – these five definitions come under this view. Almost all the philosophers except grammarians follow the Sakhaṇḍa school of sentence. The Mīmāṁsakas are of the view that sentence and sentence-meaning are produced by joining the words and the word-meanings together. There are two schools of Mīmāṁsakas, viz. Bhāṭṭa school, propounded by Kumārila Bhaṭṭa and Prābhākara school, founded by Prabhākara. The two schools have different views on the concept of sentence and sentence-meaning. Abhihitānvayavāda and Anvitābhidhānavāda are the two theories of verbal import (*śābdabodha*), held by these schools respectively.[6] Puṇyarāja, the famous commentator of the *Vākyapadīya* mentions that two among the five definitions which come within the *sakhaṇḍa* view, viz. the collection of words (*saṁghāta*) and the sequence of words (*krama*), are held by the Abhihitānvayavādins, while the other three definitions are accepted by Anvitābhidhānavādins (*Vākyapadīya* II.1-2). Thus, the first two definitions under the *sakhaṇḍa* view can be ascribed, later on, to the Bhāṭṭa school of Mīmāṁsā. The essence of the *abhihitānvaya* theory can be stated as follows: *abhihitānām padārthānām anvayaḥ*. The words in a sentence first designate their meanings and then the word-meanings are brought together to give the sentence-meaning. Though Puṇyarāja ascribes the *saṁghāta* view, to the Abhihitānvayavāda, Kumārila Bhaṭṭa, the founder of this school refutes the Saṁghātavāda in his *Ślokavārtika*.

---

[6] These theories on verbal import are expounded under subheading "Abhitānvaya and Anvitābhidhāna Theories of Sentence-Meaning" on p. 45 in this book.

evam ādyantaṁ sarveṣāṁ pr̥thak saṁghātakalpane ।
anyonyānugrahābhāvāt padānāṁ nāsti vākyatā ॥
– *Vākyādhikaraṇa* 4

He refutes Saṁghātavāda saying that the ability of words to favour each other cannot be established in a group. Bhartr̥hari criticized this view saying that just as the individual letters in a word are treated as meaningless, the individual words in a sentence also have no individual meaning.

The other three definitions under the *sakhaṇḍa* view – *ākhyāta-śabda* (verb), *padamādyam* (first word) and *pr̥thak sarvaṁ padaṁ sākāṅkṣam* (each word requiring others) – are supportive of a sort of contextualism, where the word's contextual meaning is considered to understand the sentence-meaning. This is ascribed later on to the Prābhākara school of Mīmāṁsā and also named Anvitābhidhānavāda. The idea is that a word's meaning cannot be known in isolation. When a sentence is heard, the word's contextual meaning or its meaning in connection with the meanings of other words in the sentence is understood by the hearer. In this way, each word in the sentence gives a connected sense and hence each word can convey the whole meaning of the sentence. The followers of the theory of *abhihitānvaya* believes that the sentence-meaning is the interconnection of the meanings conveyed by the individual words, while those who accept the *anvitābhidhāna* theory hold the view that sentence-meaning is not derived from the interconnection of individual words, but each word connotes a meaning that is already connected with the meanings of the others. In addition to these definitions, Bhartr̥hari also discusses the definitions of sentence by Jaimini, the founder of the Mīmāṁsā school and Kātyāyana, the author of *vārtika*s in the school of Vyākaraṇa.

Among the definitions of sentence, *jātiḥ saṁghātavartinī* (the universal inhering in the collection of words), *eko 'navayavaḥ śabdaḥ* (one individual word) and *budhyanusaṁhṛtiḥ* (unification in mind) – these definitions come under the view that sentence is indivisible (*akhaṇḍa-pakṣa*). The followers of this school consider sentence as a single unit, which has no divisions such as words or syllables. Ancient grammarians like Vyāḍi and Patañjali are in favour of this view. They accept sentence-*sphoṭa* as the minutest level of language. According to these three definitions, sentence is considered as a single unit, which cannot be taken as the group of words as in *sakhaṇḍa-pakṣa*.

All the notions of the Sakhaṇḍa school on sentence and sentence-meaning are refuted by Bhartṛhari, as they cannot explain the philosophy of sentence wholly. These definitions manifest the concept of sentence from corners only; none of them depicts a complete idea about the philosophy of sentence. Bhartṛhari sets forth instead a holistic framework and argues that a sentence might be understood as an indivisible *sphoṭa*, which is either external or internal. On a shrewd analysis of the Vākyakāṇḍa of *Vākyapadīya*, it can be concluded that Bhartṛhari never accepted the *sakhaṇḍa-pakṣa*, as he advocates syllables and words in a sentence are not real, but only imaginary.

pade na varṇā vidyante varṇeṣvavayavā na ca ।
vākyāt padānāmatyantaṁ praviveko na kaścana ॥
– *Vākyapadīya* I.68

The Concept of Sentence Indivisibility and Sphoṭa

The concept of *sphoṭa* is one of the most important contributions of Indian thinkers to the crucial problem of general linguistics. It was Bhartṛhari, who brought to light the breadth and depth of this concept beyond its linguistic features in his *Vākyapadīya*. But, some of the ideas underlying this theory can be found in earlier grammatical and philosophical literature in Sanskrit. It can be stated emphatically that, the whole superstructure of Bhartṛhari's language theory is erected on the concept of *akhaṇḍa-vākyasphoṭa*, which is already described. He used this fundamental concept in the study of language, which was successfully developed by later grammarians. This concept paved new pathways in the language studies in India. As discussed, the concept of *sphoṭa* was no new idea for the predecessors of Bhartr̥hari. But the idea of sentence-indivisibility, introduced by Bhartr̥hari, has some unique features when compared to the concept of *sphoṭa* in general. Before proceeding into the characteristics of the concept of sentence-indivisibility, Bhartr̥hari's perspectives on *sphoṭa* doctrine has to be discussed.

In the school of Grammar, the word or sentence, when taken as an indivisible meaning-unit, is the *sphoṭa*. Patañjali distinguishes *sphoṭa* and *dhvani* in his *Mahābhāṣya* as *sphoṭaḥ śabdaḥ, dhvaniḥ śabdaguṇaḥ* (vol. 1, 1991: 181). Thus *sphoṭa* is the real *śabda* (speech or language), while *dhvani*, the audible part is a quality of speech. Indologists like A.B. Keith mistakenly treated this as a mysterious entity and overlooked its linguistic significance, probably due to its association with Bhartr̥hari's *śabda-brahman* (Matilal 1992: 84). Later scholars like John Brough, Iyer and Kunjunni Raja, etc. mention *sphoṭa* as a linguistic entity. They described it as the language-symbol or an "auditory image" of the uttered speech as well as the meaning-bearing unit.[7] Matilal, examining all these views, describes *sphoṭa* as an auditory impression of the meaning (1992: 85). Bhartr̥hari begins his discussion about *sphoṭa* referring to two aspects of language:

---

7 The word *sphoṭa* is derived from the root *sphuṭa vikasane*, which signifies "to burst" or "to shine forth". Thus, it can be described in two ways: if it is explained as *sphuṭati, vikasati, arthaḥ asmāt iti sphoṭaḥ*, then *sphoṭa* is that from which the meaning shines forth and hence it can be taken as the meaning-bearing agent. If it is described as *sphuṭyate anena iti sphoṭaḥ*, then it can be defined as an entity which is manifested by the uttered speech. According to this view, *sphoṭa* is the auditory impression manifested by *dhvani*s.

dvāvupādānaśabdeṣu śabdau śabdavido viduḥ ।
eko nimittaṁ śabdānām aparo 'rthe prayujyate ॥
– *Vākyapadīya* I.44

Here, Bhartṛhari analyses the speech act from the speaker's point of view, which has two dimensions. In the language act, one is the causal root of articulated sounds (*nimittaṁ śabdānām*) while the other is the manifested or applied, to convey the meaning (*arthe prayujyate*). From the speaker's point of view, the articulated sounds are produced from the "word-principle" which is present in the intellect (*buddhisthaśabdaḥ*). Thus, the causal root of audible sound (*nāda*) is the *buddhisthaśabdaḥ* (word-principle in the intellect) (*Vākyapadīya* I.46). Bhartṛhari calls this *buddhisthaśabda* as *sphoṭa*. This gets transformed into utterance, when a person intends to speak (*Vākyapadīya* I.108). Though the uttered language is sequential, its source, the language faculty in the intellect (*buddhisthaśabdaḥ*), is devoid of any sequence or parts. But, the listener grasps the *śabda* produced by the speaker in a sequential manner, but not as a whole. Thus, he may experience the *sphoṭa* as having sequence while hearing. Bhartṛhari solves this problem by differentiating *dhvani* (audible sound) into *prākṛta-dhvani* and *vaikṛta-dhvani*.[8] The *vaikṛta-dhvani* is the actual sound spoken by the speaker and heard by the listener. Hence, it includes all the peculiarities and differences in the utterance of the speaker like intonation and tempo (Brough 1951: 40). The *prākṛta-dhvani*, which is indicated by the *vaikṛta-dhvani*, is a stage just before the articulated sounds come into existence. It represents the phonological structure or the sound pattern of the form. All the non-linguistic personal variations are absent in this stage. But, the time sequence is still present in this. This actually manifests the internal *sphoṭa*, the integral linguistic symbol. The *prākṛta-dhvani* is so close to the integral linguistic

[8] Bhartṛhari's analysis of language encompasses three aspects, viz. *vaikṛta-dhvani*, *prākṛta-dhvani* and *sphoṭa*.

symbol *sphoṭa* that the characteristics of *prākṛta-dhvani* are superimposed on *sphoṭa*. Thus, we may experience the *sphoṭa* as sequential or having parts. Brough discusses these three stages in his "Theories of General Linguistics in Sanskrit Grammar" vividly.

The later grammarians like Bhaṭṭojī Dīkṣita and Nāgeśa Bhaṭṭa enumerated eight different types of *sphoṭa*. This differentiation is based on two fundamental principles, viz. indivisibility and meaningfulness. Thus, we get *varṇa-sphoṭa*, *pada-sphoṭa* and *vākya-sphoṭa* respectively, when we consider either the letter or the word or the sentence as *vācaka* (meaning-bearing unit) (*Śabdakaustubha* 1933: 10). These three are again classified into *jāti* and *vyakti*. If word and sentence are considered as indivisible symbols denoting the meaning of the whole without any reference to the parts, they are known as *akhaṇḍa-padasphoṭa* and *akhaṇḍa-vākyasphoṭa*. These are the eight types of *sphoṭa* described by later grammarians. Though Bhartṛhari does not enumerate these eight classes of *sphoṭa*, he seems to have held the *akhaṇḍa-vākyasphoṭa* as the real *sphoṭa* (Brough 1951: 45). This is evident when he emphasizes on the definitions of sentence that come under the Akhaṇḍa school of sentence, which is already discussed. Thus, according to Bhartṛhari, the concept of *sphoṭa* in general, forms the philosophical outlook of his language theory. To Bhartṛhari, the theory of *sphoṭa* is part of his monistic and idealistic metaphysical theory according to which, the *śabda-tattva* is the eternal principle of the universe. His magnum opus *Vākyapadīya* is also begun with the statement that the whole phenomenon of material existence is only the *vivarta*[9] of this speech principle (I.1).

The concept of indivisible sentence, expounded in the second canto of *Vākyapadīya*, forms the basis of his psycholinguistic

---

[9] *Vivarta* is a concept, developed by the Advaita Vedānta system, which is described as the process of manifestation by which "one" becomes "many".

analysis of language. The idea of "sentence-indivisibility" deals with how language is used and grasped. This explains sentence as the real linguistic unit, which is devoid of any sequence or parts. Puṇyarāja points out that Bhartṛhari is not the first to introduce the idea of indivisibility in the School of Grammar. Pāṇini and Patañjali have recognized the indivisibility of sentence:

> *sūtrakārasya tu atiṅgrahaṇāt ekameva akhaṇḍaṁ vākyam*
> *arthaikatvāt ākhyātabhede 'pi abhipretamiti gamyate*
>
> – *Vākyapadīya* II.1-2

But it must be admitted that Bhartṛhari is the first to establish logically the concept of indivisibility of a sentence. He emphatically states that the sentence is "a single undivided utterance" (*eko 'navayavaḥ śabdaḥ*). Sibabjiban Bhattacharya explains this view as the phonetic completeness of the sentence and is not merely the aggregation of the words occurring in it. What is worthy of note here is that the whole sentence is an individual, and is not the aggregate of its parts (1984: 28).

The grammarians consider the sentence to be indivisible because the opposite theory of division would result in infinite regress or in the acceptance of atomism (Sharma 1998: 77). If it is held that the words in a sentence are those very ones which are found independently somewhere else and if the phonemes are those which are found independently, there would be no essence of the sentence or the words other than phonemes. If the *sakhaṇḍa* view of sentence is accepted, the phonemes also can be divided even into smaller parts like an atom and this division would be carried out infinitely. Thus ultimately, there would be no unit, which would be looked upon as the expressive element. Therefore the grammarians put forth the sentence as an entity over and above the phonemes and words.

padāni vākye tānyeva varṇāste ca pade yadi ।
varṇeṣu varṇabhāgānāṁ bhedaḥ syāt paramāṇuvat ॥
bhāgānām anupaśleṣeṇa na varṇo na padaṁ bhavet ।
teṣāmavyapadeśyatvāt kimanyadapadiśyatām ॥
– *Vākyapadīya* 2.28-29

Modern scholars like Kunjunni Raja, Brough, Iyer and Gaurinath Sastri hold that the *sphoṭa* is the auditory impression of the uttered speech as well as the meaning-bearing agent. But, this concept is not enough to solve the problem of the cognition of the sentence-meaning. Hence, they hold that the *sphoṭa* in general and *vākya-sphoṭa* in particular has been assumed as a solution to the problem of the meaning of the sentence.[10]

The Concept of Sentence-Meaning

Almost all Indian schools of thought have given primacy to the process of understanding the sentence-meaning, which is known as *śābdabodha* in their philosophies. *Śābdabodha* can be simply defined as the cognition of the meaning of a sentence. A sentence is composed of words, whether their existence is considered real as in the case of logicians, Mīmāṁsakas and others or mythical as in the case of grammarians. It is already known that words have potentiality to express definite meanings. The relation between these words that binds them to form a single sentence is the syntactical relation. Various philosophers have explored this syntactical relationship between the words in a sentence which forms various theories of *śābdabodha* (verbal import) (Rao 1969: 1).

The eight views on sentence, which are ascribed to various preceptors, follow different views on *śābdabodha*. In the *Nyāyabodhinī*

10 This view is explained under subsection "Pratibhā and the Sentence Sphoṭa" on p. 121 of this book.

which is a commentary on *Tarkasaṁgraha*, *śābdabodha* is defined as *padajñānakaraṇaṁ jñānam* (*Tarkasaṁgraha*, 1971: 39). Rao translates this as "*śābdabodha* is the cognition effected by the efficient instrumentality of the cognition of words" (1969: 2). In the *Kārikāvalī*, the Śabdakhaṇḍa begins with the verse:

padajñānaṁ tu karaṇaṁ dvāraṁ tatra padārthadhīḥ ।
śābdabodhaḥ phalaṁ tatra śaktidhīḥ sahakāriṇī ॥

– 4.81

This also gives the same idea that the cognition of the meaning of a sentence is caused by the cognition of the individual word-meanings in it. Hence to cognize the meaning of a sentence, word-meanings are to be cognized. Thus, the concept of sentence-meaning among these eight different views on sentence can be ascribed into six various views.

SIX VIEWS ON SENTENCE-MEANING

Bhartṛhari tries to converge different ideas on the concept of sentence-meaning in the second canto of *Vākyapadīya*. The definitions of sentence, discussed by Bhartṛhari, naturally point to the nature of sentence-meaning. Puṇyarāja, enumerates six views on the meaning of a sentence held by the followers of these definitions. They are *pratibhā*, *saṁsargaḥ*, *saṁsargavaśāt nirākāṅkṣo viśeṣāvasthitaḥ padārthaḥ*, *saṁsṛṣta evārthaḥ*, *kriyā* and *prayojanam* (*Vākyapadīya* II.1-2). In the Akhaṇḍa school, which perceives the sentence as indivisible into parts, the sentence-meaning is accepted as *pratibhā*. The followers of the remaining five definitions come under the Sakhaṇḍa school admit that the sentence-meaning is the result of the aggregation of individual word-meanings. These views are to be discussed elaborately.

KRIYĀ VĀKYĀRTHAḤ

For those who view sentence as the verb, meaning is in the nature of action or *kriyā*. Bhartṛhari explains this in the verse:

kriyā kriyāntarādbhinnā niyatādhārasādhanā ।
prakrāntā pratipattṛṇām bhedāḥ sambodhahetavaḥ ॥
– *Vākyapadīya* II.414

In most cases, a complete sentence contains at least a subject, predicate and verb. There are sentences which have no parts other than a verb. In anyway, the verb or the idea of an action is an inevitable part of a sentence. Bhartṛhari says that each action is different from one another as it is with specific accessories as its substrata (*niyatādhārasādhanā*). Puṇyarāja also describes the *kriyā* (action) as *viśiṣṭā*, that which is particular or qualified. Thus *kriyā* is the key factor in a sentence which differentiates it from all the other sentences. It is again mentioned in this verse that when a sentence is heard, the listener first grasps the sense of action. But it cannot be argued that the other parts in a sentence except the verb are insignificant, as they are for the vivid understanding of the listener.

Puṇyarāja quotes another verse also in his commentary, the source of which is yet to be found.

pratibhā yat prabhūtārthā yāmanuṣṭhānamāśritam ।
phalam prasūyeta yataḥ sā kriyā vākyagocaraḥ ॥
– *Vākyapadīya* II.1-2

Here it is stated that the *kriyā* in general is not to be treated as sentence-meaning. But the *kriyā*, when characterized by some qualifiers, gives the meaning of the sentence. The verb should be qualified with its accessories like *kartā* (subject) and *karma* (predicate) and should give rise to indivisible sentence-meaning *pratibhā*. This qualified verb only can stimulate action. An action cannot be taken place unless there is a subject and predicate. If one says "close", pointing towards the door, we may understand that the door is to be closed. Here the verb is impregnated with the subject and the predicate. Thus the *kriyā*, qualified with these characteristics represents the sentence-meaning. This view is a sort of word-atomism, put forth by the Anvitābhidhāna school, which says that each word in a sentence represents a connected meaning.

SAṀSARGAḤ VĀKYĀRTHAḤ

Among the definitions of sentence, those who believe sentence as the collection of words (*saṁghāta*) and as the sequence of words (*krama*), accept *saṁsarga* (interconnection) as the sentence-meaning. According to this view, sentence-meaning is the interconnection of the meanings of the individual words. This view belongs to the Abhihitānvaya school, accepted by the Bhāṭṭa school of Mīmāṁsā. This is well stated in the verse:

> *saṁbandhe sati yattvanyadādhikyam upajāyate* ।
> *vākyārthameva taṁ prāhuranekapadasaṁśrayam* ॥
> – *Vākyapadīya* II.42

When a word is connected with another in a sentence, which is mutually expected (*sākāṅkṣam*) with the first word, an extra meaning over and above the individual meanings of the words is derived. This extra meaning cannot be treated as the meanings of the words, but it is the sentence-meaning. In the expression *vīraḥ puruṣaḥ*, there are two distinct words *vīraḥ*, which denotes "courage" and *puruṣaḥ*, which signifies "a man". When these words are uttered in a way they are mutually expected (*sākāṅkṣam*), it signifies "a courageous man". This extra meaning of adjectival–substantive relation, evolved as a result of the interconnection between the word-meanings, is the sentence-meaning. This view is pointed out in the *Mahābhāṣya*, where Patañjali states that the adjectival–substantive relation is different from the individual word-meanings, but it is the sentence-meaning (*yadatrādhikyam, vākyārthaḥ saḥ*, under Patañjali II.3.46).

Bhartṛhari says that this view of sentence-meaning can be perceived in two different ways. The first view is of the universal (*jāti*), which is supposed to exist in full in each individual of the species. Similarly, if sentence is said to be the collection of words and sentence-meaning rests on many words, then the sentence-meaning exists in full in each word. The second perspective is of number, which exists in the totality of the group. In this view, the sentence-meaning rests on the totality of words (*Vākyapadīya* II.43).

SAṀSṚṢṬA EVĀRTHAḤ VĀKYĀRTHAḤ

It is an already discussed view that the sentence-meaning is *saṁsarga* (interconnection) of the meanings of the individual words. Bhartṛhari explains this view in another perspective also. In the former view, it was stated that a word in a sentence denotes its individual meaning only and when the meanings of the words are connected together, a qualified meaning emerges, which is the meaning of the sentence. Here, in this perspective, it is stated that the individual word conveys a general meaning which is potentially capable of being connected with the meanings of other words. When it is actually connected with the other words, it really conveys a meaning connected with the particular meanings of other words. This view differs from the former in the manner that, the word-meaning here, is so general and at the same time it is adaptable to all the particulars. The general meaning and the particular meaning are those of the individual word and not of the sentence and is not conveyed by *ākāṅkṣā*, *yogyatā* and *sannidhi* (*Vākyapadīya* II.44-46). What is peculiar to this view is that the *saṁghāta* view is explained here from the point of view of the school of Anvitābhidhāna.

VIŚEṢARŪPĀPANNAḤ PADĀRTHAḤ EVA VĀKYĀRTHAḤ

Those who define the sentence as "the first word" (*padamādyam*) and "each word requiring the others" (*pṛthak sarvam padam sākāṅkṣam*) accept sentence-meaning as the connected meaning. According to them, the whole of the sentence meaning is concentrated in each word (*Vākyapadīya* II.18). But here, we may doubt if the other words in the sentence are of no use. Bhartṛhari solves this problem, saying that, the other words are not useless, but they make listeners understand the meaning better. If in the very beginning, a connected meaning involving an action and all its accessories is understood, why the accessories, restated in the sentence, are also explained by Bhartṛhari? It is for specifying the substrata of the powers of the accessories (*Vākyapadīya* II.411-12, tr. Iyer).

PRAYOJANAṀ VĀKYĀRTHAḤ

Puṇyarāja states that for some, the sentence-meaning is *prayojanam* (is in the nature of purpose). This is supposed to be common to all the views on the nature of sentence-meaning. According to this view, the sentence-meaning is neither derived from the interconnection of the meanings of individual words as in the school of Abhihitānvaya, nor is the connected meaning of each word as in the school of Anvitābhidhāna. Here, the word-meaning is the expressed sense and the sentence denotes purpose. What is understood on hearing a sentence is nothing but *abhidheya* (expressed sense). The sentence-meaning is the purpose, which fulfils the speaker's intention:

> *abhidheyaḥ padasyārtho vākyasyārthaḥ prayojanam* ।
> *yasya tasya na sambandho vākyānāmupapadyate* ॥
> – *Vākyapadīya* II.113

The definition of sentence, propounded by Jaimini, who authored the *sūtra*s of Mīmāṁsā, also supports this view. He defines sentence in the aphorism:

> *arthaikatvādekam vākyam sākāṅkṣam ced vibhāge syāt*
> – II.1.46

In this aphorism, the term *arthaikatva* is explained by Śabara (*Mīmāṁsā darśanam* 1984) in the sense of "serving a single purpose" (*ekaprayojanatvādupapannam*, Jaimini 2.1.46). Later Mīmāṁsakas like Kumārila Bhaṭṭa and Pārthasārathi Miśra, also favour this view.

Bhartr̥hari refutes this view, pointing out its defects. He says that if the sentence has no *abhidheya* (expressed meaning), there would be no connection between sentences. Such connection is established only through the expressed meaning. He also mentions that this defect can be removed or solved according to the concept of *anvitābhidhāna* (*Vākyapadīya* II.113).

PRATIBHĀ VĀKYĀRTHAḤ

Bhartr̥hari emphasizes on the Akhaṇḍa school of sentence, which holds the indivisibility of the sentence and the sentence-meaning. Bhartr̥hari termed this all-inclusive and indivisible sentence-meaning as *pratibhā*. In the *akhaṇḍa-pakṣa*, sentence-meaning is not derived from the meanings of words in it. Bhartr̥hari introduces the concept of *pratibhā* in the following verse:

> *vicchedagrahaṇe 'rthānāṁ pratibhānyaiva jāyate* ।
> *vākyārtha iti tāmāhuḥ padārthairupapāditām* ॥
> – *Vākyapadīya* II.143

When the meanings of the individual words in a sentence have been understood separately, a flash of understanding takes place. This is the meaning of the sentence, brought about by the meanings of the individual words. In the school of Sentence-Indivisibility, though individual words and their meanings are considered unreal, they serve the purpose of bringing the sentence-meaning to the mind. In other words, they manifest the sentence-meaning. The listener receives the uttered sounds in a sequential manner and hence the meanings of the parts of a sentence may be perceived in the listener's mind. But as soon as a sentence, the complete linguistic unit, is perceived, a sudden flash of understanding takes place. This flash of understanding is termed as *pratibhā*. The whole semantic exposition of Bhartṛhari has been developed on this unique as well as original concept.

VARIOUS MEANS OF ASCERTAINMENT OF MEANING

According to Bhartṛhari, sentence is the primary conveyor of meaning in a communication. Words and word-meanings are only manifesters of the meaning of sentence. In certain situations, word-meanings are even insignificant also. Bhartṛhari says that to console a crying child, one may threaten him that a tiger would eat him. Here, the intention of the speaker is not to threaten the child, but to put off his crying (*Vākyapadīya* II.321). Sometimes, the intention may be far away from the chief meaning of the sentence. Bhartṛhari cites some examples for such ambiguities in the meaning. When one says to other "look at the sun, we have to go", it really indicates the time, even though it says something about sun (*Vākyapadīya* II.310). Similarly, when a boy is told "save the butter from the crows", the speaker intends to keep the butter away from all the birds and animals. Thus, Bhartṛhari intends to say that the meaning of a sentence does not depend on the meanings of its parts. But it is a flash of understanding. Speakers use the words to express the literal sense and also to express some intended sense. The speaker's intention, embedded in the sentence, cannot be understood through its parts. Bhartṛhari says that the meanings of words are determined according to the sentence, situation, meaning, propriety, place and time, but not according to its mere external form.

> *vākyāt prakaraṇādarthaucityāddeśakālataḥ* ।
> *śabdārthāḥ pravibhajyante na rūpādeva kevalāt* ॥
> – *Vākyapadīya* II.314

Besides these factors, he gives an account of contextual and syntactic factors, which helps to determine the precise meaning of an expression. They are stated in the following verses:

saṁsargo viprayogaśca sāhacaryaṁ virodhitā ı
arthaṁ prakaraṇaṁ liṅgam śabdasyānyasya sannidhiḥ ıı

sāmarthyamaucitī deśaḥ kālo vyaktiḥ svarādayaḥ ı
śabdārthasyānavacchede viśeṣasmṛtihetavaḥ ıı
– *Vākyapadīya* II.315-16

Vṛtti and the commentary of Puṇyarāja make this view clear by citing examples. Iyer opines that these verses may be quotations from some unknown work (*Vākyapadīya* II.314). Anyway this list has been adopted by the later philosophers to discuss about the problems of ambiguous expressions.

i. *Saṁyoga* (Association): Some words are used in more than one meaning. The meaning in which it is used in a particular context can be determined by its association with other words. The word *hari* can be taken as the example. This word is used to denote various meanings like "Lord Viṣṇu", "monkey" and "lion". When this word is associated with the words *śaṅkha* (conch) and *cakra* (discus), it denotes Lord Viṣṇu.

ii. *Viprayoga* (Dissociation): The meaning of words, which denotes more than one meaning, can be determined by dissociation also. The sentence *akiśorā dhenurānīyatām* is the given example. The word *dhenu* may denote a "cow" or a "mare". But here, the phrase *akiśorā* (without calf) implies dissociation, which makes it clear that a cow is referred to.

iii. *Sāhacaryam* (Mutual Association): When somebody says "Rāma and Lakṣmaṇa went to forest", it is unambiguous that the son of Daśaratha is referred to here, but not Balarāma (the brother of Kṛṣṇa). This meaning is determined on the basis of mutual association of Rāma with Lakṣmaṇa.

iv. *Virodhitā* (Opposition): It is stated that the word Rāma refers to the son of Daśaratha when associated with the word Lakṣmaṇa. Similarly when the same word Rāma is used in the compound word Rāmārjunau (Rāma and Arjuna), it obviously denotes Paraśurāma (incarnation of Lord Viṣṇu). It is because of the hostility between Paraśurāma and Kārtavīryārjuna.

v. *Arthaḥ* (Purpose): The word *sthāṇu* means a "pillar" or "Lord Śiva". When someone is asked to "worship *sthāṇu*", the purpose of the speaker is to worship "Lord Śiva", not the pillar. Thus the purpose of the speaker helps the listener to determine the latter meaning of the term.

vi. *Prakaraṇam* (Context): The well-known example is the expression *saindhavam ānaya*, in which the word *saindhavam* signifies both "salt" and "horse". Here, the meaning is determined by the context. If it is the time of eating, the term denotes "salt" and it denotes "horse" at the time of travel.

vii. *Liṅga* (Indicatory Sign): Matilal explains this as follows: "some sign may be present in the larger context (within the passage), and this may help to resolve the ambiguity" (1992: 25). An example is taken from a Vedic passage, which reads as *aktāḥ śarkarā upadadhāti* (the wet pebbles are placed on the altar). Here, the word *aktāḥ* signifies "wet". To make the pebbles wet, they can be soaked in any liquid, because it is not specified in the sentence. Since the context mentions "clarified butter", we have to understand that it is an indicatory sign that the pebbles should be made wet by the clarified butter.

viii. *Śabdasyānyasya sannidhiḥ* (Proximity with Another Word): This is also a sort of association, but differs from *sāhacaryam* or *virodhitā*. Here, it is not the psychological association as in the case of *sāhacaryam* or *virodhitā*, but perhaps a physical proximity or a syntactical connection is meant (Matilal 1992: 26). The example given by Matilal is the word *purārāti*, which literally means "destroyer of cities". Though any king can be denoted by the word, it obviously refers to "Lord Śiva".

ix. *Sāmarthya* (Capacity): When one says *abhirūpāya kanyā deyā*, it is clear that the girl has to be married to a handsome groom. Though the word groom is not said by the speaker, the listener understands it. Similarly when one says "I am intoxicated with *madhu*", the word *madhu* would mean wine, not the spring season.

x. *Aucitī* (Propriety): This is a variation of the former concept. In a poetic context, the same word *madhu* can also signify the spring season. In that particular situation, it may be proper to say "I am intoxicated with the advent of the spring season".

xi. *Deśa* (Place): In the expression *bhātīha parameśvaraḥ*, which means "here shines the master", the word *parameśvara* signifies "the king" and not "Lord Śiva". The reference to the place "here" helps to attribute this meaning to the term.

xii. *Kāla* (Time): When one says "*citrabhānu* shines now", the word *citrabhānu* refers to the sun if it is said at daytime and it refers to fire or light if it is uttered at night.

xiii. *Vyakti* (Grammatical Gender): It is well known that the term *mitra* in Sanskrit signifies "sun" when it is used in masculine gender. And the same word means "friend", if it is used in neuter gender.

xiv. *Svara* (Accent): A well-known example is cited in the *Mahābhāṣya* that the word *indraśatru* with accent on the last syllable means "one who kills Indra". When the first syllable of the word is accented, it means "the one, whose killer is Indra". Thus in the Veda, a word may denote a different or opposite meaning if the accent used is improper.

These are the contextual factors that help one determine the meaning of an expression unambiguously. Bhartṛhari says that even many more factors are there, which influence the meaning of a word. Thus, it is obvious that Bhartṛhari takes into account the grammatical, syntactical, psychological and contextual factors for determining the intended meaning. These factors are not related to a specific language, but they are universal in nature. Thus it becomes clear that he deals with the problems of communicability of language and word-meaning relationship in a comprehensive manner.

4

The Concept of Pratibhā and Its Implications

Origin and Development of the Concept of Pratibhā

THE CONCEPT of *pratibhā* is discussed elaborately in almost all schools of thought in India and the preceptors perceive this concept in different dimensions. Normally, in Indian philosophy, the concept of *pratibhā* might be conceived as the "supersensuous and suprarational apperception for grasping the truth directly" (Rath 2000: 141). Even though there are a few references to the term *pratibhā* in Vedic literature, we can trace the concept in the *R̥gveda* and *Nirukta*. In the *R̥gveda*, the term *pratibhā* is referred to as *pratibabhau* (*tritam kūpe 'vahitam etat sūktaṁ pratibabhau*, I.105.17). Here, the word *pratibabhau* denotes revelation or a quick understanding of insight or a sudden thought (Rath 2000: 142). In *Nirukta*, it is stated as *pratibabhau*, which signifies "it was revealed". Yāska uses the word in a different sense also as "image", "light" or "splendour" (2002: 4.6; 14.4).

The word *pratibhā* is etymologically derived from the root *bhā*, which means "to shine" (*dīptau*). The prefix *prati* and the suffixes *kaḥ* and *ṭāp* are added to the root. The suffix *kaḥ* is added in the sense of either *karma* or *bhāva*. Hence, the meaning of the word *pratibhā* can be taken as *pratibhāti*, *śobhate iti pratibhā* (to shine) or *pratibhāti arthaḥ anayā iti sā pratibhā* (that which gives the meaning). Dasgupta remarks:

> In its ordinary non-technical use, the term *pratibhā* refers to an intuition of what may occur in future. It also includes the power of understanding of all kinds of sounds without effort, all that may be communicated by any animal in the world and the power of having heavenly visions. – 1975: 342

Various Indian schools of thought used this concept in their technical discussions in different dimensions. It may be discussed here at some length, and afterwards, Bhartṛhari's conception of *pratibhā* will be discussed elaborately.

The Concept of Pratibhā in Indian Philosophy

In general, Indian schools of thought use the term *pratibhā* as a concept which indicates any kind of knowledge, which is not sense-borne. As it implies a supersensuous knowledge, the prime characters of this concept are immediacy and intense clarity. Hence it is described as a flash or the sense of wisdom characterized by immediacy and freshness (*nanvonmeṣaśālinī prajñā*). It is because of the supersensuous nature, *pratibhā* is transcendental and non-empirical. It is always free from the limitations of time and space. In this sense, it is rather equivalent to intuition. In Indian systems of thought, the concept of *pratibhā* is described both as an inherent power and as an act of voluntary consciousness (Rath 2000: 141). As an inherent power of wisdom, it can be sublimated to the intuitive knowledge of the self. As an act, it has the capacity to put someone into creative forms such as poetry or art. Thus, Padma Sudhi puts forth:

> *Pratibhā*, as the intuitive knowledge, gives expressions to the art forms as talent or genius. Thus artistic talent or genius is nothing but *pratibhā* and its spiritual quest. – 1983, vol. III: 124

In short, the concept of *pratibhā* is omnipresent in all novel ideas in any area of science, art, literature, philosophy, etc. In other words, they are inspired by *pratibhā*.

In one way or other, almost all Indian philosophies have included this supersensuous knowledge or intuition in their technical discussions. The doctrine of *pratibhā*, in the same form or other, has ever been an article of universal acceptance in India. Except Cārvākas, all other philosophers describe a supernatural perception, which enables one to directly grasp the real nature of things. Most of these schools may not name this unique perception as *pratibhā*, but the schools of Yoga, Vedānta and Buddhism exclusively discuss the characteristics of it. Cārvāka system, being a materialistic philosophy, denies any sort of supernatural perception. According to them, sense perception is the only source of knowledge. Harold Coward opines that in the Cārvāka system, everything is derived from material elements which are judged to possess their own *svabhāva* (immanent life force) (1980: 50). It has to be noted that Bhartṛhari recognizes *pratibhā* as *svabhāvaja* (*pratibhā*, that derives from the *svabhāva* or nature), while describing the six kinds of it[1] (*Vākyapadīya* II.152). Thus, the omnipresence of *pratibhā* in the Cārvāka school cannot be denied completely. In Jainism, we may find no direct reference to this concept. Still they implicitly discuss similar notions while they describe the concept of *avadhi-jñāna* or *kevala-jñāna*. The followers of Pūrva-Mīmāṁsā school do not accept any kind of supernatural perception and therefore they refute the *pratibhā* theory. But Kumārila, in his *Ślokavārtika*, invokes *Mahādeva* (Supreme Being), who possesses a *Divya Cakṣus* (Divine Eye) in the form of three Vedas (1). Here, the *Divya Cakṣus* (Divine Eye), which has a capacity of supernatural perception, in its essence, is equivalent to *pratibhā*. There is no direct reference of

---

[1] Six kinds of *pratibhā* are explicated under section "Pratibhā: Its Sources" on p. 116.

this concept in the Sāṁkhya philosophy also. But we may find some description of intuitional consciousness while discussing about *kaivalya* (Prasad 2010: 17). Nyāya philosophy also uses this term to signify the intuitive consciousness from which, fresh and novel ideas are awakened. M.B. Jhalakikar points out that the concept is defined in the Nyāya school as *sphūrtyākhyo buddhiviśeṣah* ("a special mode of forming and retaining conceptions of the quivering or sudden appearance of description", tr. Rath 2000: 147) or *prajñā navanavonmeṣaśālinī pratibhā matā* (intuitive consciousness abounding in always new awakenings, quoted in Rath 2000: 147).

Yoga discusses the concept of *pratibhā* exclusively so as to describe the supernatural perception or omniscience that a *yogī* attains in contemplation. Here, the term *prajñā* is often used in the sense of *pratibhā*. The most significant reference is seen in the third chapter of Patañjali's *Yogasūtra*, which states that *pratibhādvā sarvam* (III.33). One who practises *yoga* can attain the real nature of all because of *pratibhā* or the innate capacity. Here, *pratibhā* is described as a spontaneous flash of insight, which is awakened with the practice of concentration. This state is termed as *sasmita samādhi*, in which, one becomes self-conscious as well as "all-conscious". Once *pratibhā* is awakened, one attains the power of supernormal perception of hearing, touch, sight, taste and awareness of events of the subtle, concealed, remote, whether past or future.

> *prātibhaṁ nāma tārakam* । *tadvivekajasya jñānasya pūrvarūpam* ।
> *tena vā sarvameva jānāti yogī prātibhasya jñānasyotpattāviti* ।
> – *Vyāsabhāṣya* 3.33

Thus, in the Yoga school, all sorts of omniscience can be explained through this unique concept of *pratibhā* and hence it is considered as an important thesis by the followers of this school.

The word *pratibhā* is seen in earlier Buddhist literature itself. The *Aṅguttara Nikāya*, one of the oldest canonical works of

Buddhists, refers to four types of poets, among which the last one is *pratibhānakavi* (quoted in Rath 2000: 147). We can assume that the *pratibhā* theory of Bhartr̥hari influenced Diṅnāga, the famous Buddhist logician. He mentions in his *Pramāṇasamuccayavr̥tti* that meaning of a sentence is *pratibhā* under the influence of *Vākyapadīya*.[2]

> *apoddhāre padasyāyaṁ vākyād artho vivecitaḥ* ।
> *vākyārthaḥ pratibhākhyo yaṁ tenādāvupajanyate* ॥
> – Quoted in Coward and Raja 2008: 28 n 26

The Concept of Pratibhā in Indian Poetics

The concept of *pratibhā* as a source of innovative and fresh ideas has been placed at its core by rhetoricians in their literary theories. The semantic as well as psychological study of *pratibhā* by Bhartr̥hari, the famous philosopher-cum-linguist, inspired rhetoricians much. Bhartr̥hari's conception of *pratibhā* as eternal, undivided and of the nature of continuous intuition has given a new perspective to the rhetoricians to pave new pathways in Alaṁkāraśāstra. Almost all the preceptors of the school of Poetics in India have tried to define this concept in various perspectives. In general, Alaṁkāraśāstra has taken it as the root of all poetic creations. It is an intuition or intellect of a poet from where fresh and creative sparks are bloomed. It is the power of intellect whereby the poet sees the subjects of his poem as steeped in beauty and gives a vivid and beautiful picture of what he has seen.

---

[2] Many scholars of modern times have rightly observed the indebtedness of Diṅnāga to Bhartr̥hari in his main work *Pramāṇasamuccayavr̥tti*. He quotes three verses of the *Vākyapadīya* in this work to support his arguments.Quoted in Coward and Raja Masaaki Hattori argues that the Buddhist theory of language, *anyāpoha*, resembles Bhartr̥hari's concept of *jāti* discussed in the Jātisamuddeśa of *Vākyapadīya* (Coward and Raja 2008: 27).

This innate capacity of a poet has been called in various names such as *pratibhā* and *śakti* in Indian poetics. In the *Kāvyālaṁkāra*, Bhāmaha states that *kāvyaṁ tu jāyate jātu kasyacit pratibhāvataḥ* (1.5). He opines that *pratibhā* is the most important equipment for a poet to compose poetry. Later preceptors of poetics also maintain almost the same view as of Bhāmaha. Rudraṭa, who also authored a work named *Kāvyālaṁkāra*, calls it as *śakti*, which is characterized by extraordinary innate attribute of soul and poetic imagination shines forth on it (1.15). Vāmana, a prominent Ālaṁkārika in the pre-Dhvani period, emphasizes in his treatise *Kāvyālaṁkārasūtravṛtti* that *pratibhā* is the sole cause of poetry. His perspective of *pratibhā* is clear in these words:

> *kavitābījaṁ pratibhānaṁ, yasmāt vinā kāvyaṁ na niṣpadyate, niṣpannaṁ vā hāsyāyatanaṁ syāt* ǀ – 1.3.16

The germ of poetry is *pratibhā*, in the absence of which, poetry does not originate and even if composed, it will be ridiculed by the society.

Ānandavardhana, the foremost thinker in Indian poetics as well as the founder of Dhvani school of Literary Criticism, has given a prime position to the concept of *pratibhā* in his magnum opus *Dhvanyāloka*. He was much influenced by Bhartṛhari's perspectives of *pratibhā* as well as *sphoṭa*. Bhartṛhari's concept of *pratibhā* is all-inclusive that the scope of this concept reaches all the aspects of universal activities. Ānandavardhana restricts this concept to the poetic imagination and extends its scope in the realm of aesthetics and poetics. Thus, he acknowledges the indebtedness to the views of the grammarians in developing the theory of *dhvani* (*prathame hi vidvāṁso vaiyākaranāḥ* – *Dhvanyāloka* 2006: 138). Ānandavardhana builds up his whole theses of literary criticism with the *pratibhā* at its core. He and the followers of the school of Dhvani reiterate the supremacy of imagination and *rasa* in their theses. Poet's imagination is deeply rooted in *pratibhā* or it is the manifestation of *pratibhā*. It needs no external guidance or requirements to manifest the poetry. This can also be equated with the famous definition of poetry by William Wordsworth as "all good poetry is the spontaneous overflow of powerful emotions" (Brett and Jones 1963: 266). Ānandavardhana views that without *pratibhā*, poetry cannot be composed. He also adds that *pratibhā* can make up the lack of learning or scholarship, but the lacking of *pratibhā* can be substituted by none. *Pratibhā* as a poetic flash transforms an ordinary man into a poet having a vision (*darśana*). It is said that a seer (*ṛṣi*) having a *darśana* only can be a poet. Rhetoricians have no dispute among them in the view that a poet should be capable of expressing that which he "sees" (*varṇanānipuṇaḥ*). But this poetic expression flashes forth only with the help of *darśana* or *pratibhā*, as mentioned.

According to Rājaśekhara, *pratibhā* is the creative faculty of the poet as well as the reader. He conceives *pratibhā* in two ways: *kārayitrī* and *bhāvayitrī* respectively. Thus, earlier as well as later rhetoricians accept *pratibhā* as the inherent wonderful faculty of natural disposition and inborn gift of the poet (Rath 2000: 149). In other words, it is the intelligent faculty of intellect where new and novel blooming of ideas arise.

The Concept of Pratibhā in Vākyapadīya

As discussed, *sphoṭa* is the auditory impression of the sentence uttered and *pratibhā* is its meaning. According to Bhartṛhari, sentence is the basic meaningful unit in a communication and we understand the meaning as a flash of understanding in the light of *pratibhā*. The sentence theory of Bhartṛhari is to be understood from the context of his general theory of knowledge, *pratibhā*. Bhartṛhari defines the very concept as:

vicchedagrahaṇe 'rthānām pratibhānyaiva jāyate ।
vākyārtha iti tāmāhuḥ padārthairupapāditām ॥
– *Vākyapadīya* II.143

When the meanings of the individual words in a sentence are understood separately, a flash of understanding takes place, which is different from the word-meanings and is called sentence-meaning. This meaning is brought about by the meanings of the individual words, but at the same time, it is unique as well as devoid of parts. Each utterance reveals the *sphoṭa* (an auditory impression) while *pratibhā* immediately translates it into meaning. Bhartṛhari conceives the concept of *pratibhā* in a unique manner that he envisages it both semantically and psychologically. *Pratibhā* in the semantic perspective is the sentence-meaning. From the psychological point of view, it may be perceived as an "intuitive instinct", which has intuitive powers ranging from instinctive knowledge of animals or birds to supernatural perceptions of *yogīs*.

Characteristics of Pratibhā

Bhartṛhari expounds the characteristic features of this concept in several verses. He states that though *pratibhā* is experienced by everyone within himself, it cannot be explained to others as "it is this". Even the subject, who experienced it, is not able to render an account of it to himself.

idaṁ taditi sānyeṣāmanākhyeyā kathañcana ।
pratyātmavṛttisiddhā sā kartrāpi na nirūpyate ॥
– *Vākyapadīya* II.144

K.A.S. Iyer explains this verse by citing an example of a drink made up of many ingredients. It is difficult to explain the taste of such a drink to others, even by the one who tastes it (*Vākyapadīya* II.146). Thus, Bhartṛhari calls the *pratibhā* as *avicārita* (indefinable).

upaśleṣamivārthānāṁ sā karotyavicāritā ।
sārvarūpyamivāpannā viṣayatvena vartate ॥
– *Vākyapadīya* II.145

Puṇyarāja explains that this flash of understanding brings about an amalgamation (*upaśleṣa*) of the meanings of the individual words, which were not connected before (*asaṁsṛṣṭa*).

Bhartṛhari suggests that *pratibhā* would be revealed when the speech faculty comes into action. *Pratibhā* is produced either through the words or through the *bhāvanā*, one's predispositions.

sākṣācchabdena janitāṁ bhāvanānugamena vā ।
itikartavyatāyāṁ tāṁ na kaścidativartate ॥
– *Vākyapadīya* II.146

Thus, there are two possibilities in the production of *pratibhā*. If it is manifested by the uttered speech, it can be produced here and it should be inherited from previous births, if produced by *bhāvanā*. Bhartṛhari argues that none can avoid its presence in his/her activities. *Pratibhā* motivates each and every activity. People indulge it in their activities only when they are motivated either by mental stimulation or from the previous impressions acquired (even from previous births). A mental stimulation is the idea originated in the mind or inspired by the audible sounds. What is worthy of note here is that the flash of understanding is always preceded by the linguistic faculty (*śabda-bhāvanā*).

Pratibhā is the cause of any sentient being indulged in any activity. In other words, any action in this world presupposes a will to act. When it is impregnated with words, it becomes cognizable by the listener. Thus Bhartṛhari opines that the whole world considers *pratibhā* as an authority.

pramāṇatvena tāṁ lokaḥ sarvaḥ samanuśyati ।
samārambhāḥ pratāyante tiraścāmapi tadvaśāt ॥
– *Vākyapadīya* II.147

No activity of a living being is possible without the precedence of *pratibhā*. Bhartṛhari argues that *pratibhā* is the reason behind the transformation of the voice of male cuckoo during the spring season. The same *pratibhā* teaches animals and birds to build nests. *Pratibhā* motivates the stimulations of hunger, thirst, love, etc. in animals and birds (*Vākyapadīya* II.148-51). Here, Bhartṛhari says that *pratibhā* or *śabda* is present in every living being by birth itself. In living beings other than human beings, it is not fully developed. In new born babies, it is the reason behind their communication through crying, laughing, etc. They cannot speak, only because their speech organs are not mature enough.

PRATIBHĀ: A SEMANTIC CONCEPT

Pratibhā is the semantic unit of communication, where sentence-meaning shines forth. The semantic characteristics of *pratibhā* have been glimpsed elaborately in the previous chapter (under subsection "Pratibhā Vākyārthaḥ" on p. 94). The whole discussions of Bhartṛhari on sentence-meaning is to be understood on the basis of the concept of *pratibhā* elucidated by him. *Sphoṭa* and *pratibhā* are the two major linguistic components underlying the syntactico–semantic analysis of sentence in the *Vākyapadīya*.

> According to Bhartṛhari, sentence is the meaningful linguistic unit. Every expression consists of three elements, i.e. *dhvani* (*nāda* or the physical sound), *sphoṭa* (intermediary mental word) and *artha* (meaning). – Rath 2000: 149

Thus, apart from the physical sound *dhvani* and the intermediary auditory image *sphoṭa*, there is another knowledge which prevails in the intellect. This transforms *sphoṭa* into meaning in a flash and is known as *pratibhā*. This transformation takes place so fast that the gap between the flash and the understanding of the sentence-meaning cannot be noticed.

PRATIBHĀ: INDIVISIBILITY OF MEANING

Bhartṛhari advocates that sentence cannot be divided into smaller parts, rather it is a single unit. Modern scholars also suggest that the whole expression should be taken into account in a conversation to understand the meaning. Bhartṛhari's Akhaṇḍa school considers sentence as a unified whole, which cannot be derived from its parts, viz. words or syllables (*Vākyapadīya* I.73). Though the words in a sentence are grasped successively, the perception of the sentence is simultaneous, when the meaning is flashed in the listener's mind (Raja 1962: 134-35).

According to the Akhaṇḍa school, *pratibhā* is also devoid of parts or sequence. It cannot be divided into word-meanings. In other words, sentence-meaning is not evolved as a result of the summation of individual meanings of the components. Mīmāṁsakas as well as Naiyāyikas, who belong to the Sakhaṇḍa school, advocate that the sentence-meaning is evolved from the word-meanings. Here, word is considered as the unit of meaning and not a product of sentence analysis. According to Bhartṛhari, the concept of sentence can be perceived from both the levels of communication and grammar. In the level of communication, sentence is the meaningful unit of language and is a unified whole or devoid of components. Sentence-meaning is also grasped as a whole by the hearer. Thus words and word-meanings have no independent status in communicating a thought or an idea. While sentence is analysed for the purpose of grammatical studies, words are only abstracted from the sentence (*apoddhāra*). In linguistics and grammar, words and word-meanings abstracted from sentence have great importance. Thus, according to Bhartṛhari, components of a sentence are significant only for studying grammar (*śāstra vyavahāra*) and they have no independent status in communication.

As the sentence-meaning *pratibhā* is grasped as a whole, it lacks any sequential nature. Bhartṛhari states that *śabda*, which is devoid of divisions, is also devoid of any sequence (*Vākyapadīya* I.48). To quote A.N. Hota:

> According to Bhartṛhari, sequence which belongs to the phonological act is imposed upon time. Intellect gets expanded along with sequence of sounds it perceives and so sequence leaves its marking on intellect. Intellect has a dual ability, namely to grasp wholes with or without sequence, and so becomes capable of perceiving one object in "singleness" and diversity. Lastly, since sounds appear in our notion with a sequence, the meaning which comes from sounds also appear to have a sequence in our notion, although it is indivisible. These are presuppositions for understanding the character of meaning. – 1985: 143

EXTRALINGUAL MEANING

Bhartṛhari rightly observes that apart from the ordinary meaning, sentences express some extralingual meanings very often in verbal communication (*Vākyapadīya* II.310-13). Some philosophers call it as *lakṣaṇa* (secondary meaning), which is either depending upon speaker's intention or on contextual factors. Even though sentence is considered as the meaningful unit of language, in most of the cases, a sentence cannot be analysed apart from the context in which it is uttered. The circumstances, in which the communication takes place, obviously influence the meaning. Here, the word "context" includes not just the environmental surroundings of the speaker, but it signifies several factors that help the hearer to fix the meaning. Bhartṛhari refers to a list of several factors which influence the meaning of a sentence (*Vākyapadīya* II.316-17) and these are elucidated in the previous chapter. Thus, the coalescence of word-meanings cannot determine the sentence-meaning. This supports the indivisibility theory of sentence-meaning.

The Vyākaraṇa school accepts only the primary sense which is based on lexical meaning. But even in the conversations of our daily life, we use expressions and phrases whose meaning cannot be understood by knowing the sentence-meaning or word-meanings. In these situations, the primary sense fails to convey the meaning of the expression. Philosophies like Nyāya and Vedānta as well as the school of Alaṁkāraśāstra accept several levels of meanings beyond the lexical meaning like *lakṣyārtha* (secondary meaning), *vyaṅgyārtha* (suggestive meaning), *tātparyārtha* and *prakaraṇārtha*. They are the extralingual meanings which are over and above the ordinary meanings of the sentence. Bhartṛhari's concept of *pratibhā* includes these infinite levels of meaning that shine forth from a conversation.

PRATIBHĀ: AN INTUITIVE INSTINCT

Bhartṛhari emphasizes that nobody can avoid *pratibhā* in one's activities, which is produced either through words or through *bhāvana*.

> *sākṣācchabdena janitāṁ bhāvanānugamena vā* ।
> *itikartavyatāyāṁ tāṁ na kaścidativartate* ॥
> – *Vākyapadīya* II.146

Each and every activity of living beings is preceded by this intuitive knowledge. In communication, it is produced by the words while it is born with a predisposition (*itikartavyatā*) in the case of children or animals. The day-to-day activities of all animals develop because of this *pratibhā*. It is not only comprehension or manifestation of an idea, but also the knowledge of how to act. Here, *pratibhā* is conceived at the level of instincts of animals and birds. As we know, all animals have a tendency to act according to the nature of their classes of beings. Sometimes they tend to act in response to the stimulations from the outer environment also. But from where does this tendency arise, is the central problem. Zoologists as well as psychologists show their interest in this field. They suggest that animals act according to their instincts. Without instincts the organism would be an inert lifeless mass only. They are the motivators and shapers of all individuals and their social life. Instincts are inborn complex patterns of behaviour that exist in most members of the species. Any behaviour is instinctive if it is performed without being based upon prior experience, and is therefore an expression of innate biological factors. Sea turtles, newly hatched on a beach will automatically move towards the ocean. Communication of honeybees by dancing in the direction of food source is another example. Other examples include animal fighting, animal courtship behaviour, internal escape functions and the building of nests. In general, it is defined as:

> largely inheritable and unalterable tendency of an organism to make a complex and specific response to environmental stimuli without involving reason.
>
> – https://www.merriam-webster.com/instinct.

These instincts or behaviour patterns are inherited or inborn and are manifested in response to certain stimuli.

Bhartṛhari tries to answer these complex behaviours and instincts of animals through the concept of *pratibhā*. He remarks that intuitions are produced just as some substances acquire the power to intoxicate without the help of any external efforts. According to him, *pratibhā* is an intuitive knowledge and this transforms the voice of the male cuckoo in spring season as well as teaches animals to build nests, etc. *Pratibhā* stimulates animals and birds on to actions like eating, loving, fighting and swimming associated with particular species (*Vākyapadīya* II.148-50, tr. Iyer). Puṇyarāja compares this intuition to the conscience of good people (*sajjana*), which enables them to decide what is right and what is wrong quite instinctively. To support this argument, he also quotes Kālidāsa's famous verse:

> *satām hi sandehapadeṣu vastuṣu pramāṇamantaḥkaraṇa-pravṛttayaḥ* ।
>
> – *Vākyapadīya* II.147

Kālidāsa tries to convey the idea that "for good people, their own conscience is the guiding force or authority, in matters of doubt". Puṇyarāja remarks that these intuitions are caused by predispositions, peculiar to every living being of different species and these are deeply rooted in the intuitive knowledge, *pratibhā*.

Bhartṛhari again puts forth an idea that this intuition is the result of *āgama* (tradition), accompanied by *bhāvanā*.

> *bhāvanānugatād etad āgamād eva jāyate* ।
> *āsattiviprakarṣābhyām āgamastu viśiṣyate* ॥
> – *Vākyapadīya* II.151

In this verse, the words *āgama*, *bhāvanā*, *āsatti* and *viprakarṣa* are not clear. It is difficult to decide what Bhartṛhari meant by these words. Puṇyarāja understands the word *āgama* as *śabda* (word). Therefore, *śabda*, either proximate or remote, is the cause of intuition. *Bhāvanā* is the tendency to act according to the nature of different classes of beings. Thus, *pratibhā* arises from *āgama*, which is assisted by *bhāvanā*. Raghunatha Sarma explains this verse as:

> *bhāvanāsahakāreṇa pratibhāyā hetubhūtaḥ āgamaḥ dvividhaḥ-āsanno viprakṛṣṭaśca* । *tatrāsanna iha janmani, viprakṛṣṭo janmāntare ityevamāsattiviprakarṣābhyām śabda eva pratibhāheturiti* । – *Vākyapadīya* II.151

It gets clear from this explanation, that the word (*śabda*) is the root of *pratibhā*. It is proximate if it arises in this very life and is remote when it is inherited from the previous births. K.A.S. Iyer has some pertinent suggestions in this regard. He doubts when Puṇyarāja says that the word *āgama* signifies *śabda*, whether he has the words of Veda in mind. Similarly, by the word *bhāvanā*, does Bhartṛhari mean what he calls *śabda-bhāvanā* in *Vākyapadīya* I.114 (*Vākyapadīya* II.151, tr. Iyer, 63). Bhartṛhari's theory of *śabda-brahman* can also be conjoined here. He says:

na so 'sti pratyayoloke yaḥ śabdānugamādṛte |
anuviddhamiva jñānam sarvam śabdena bhāsate ||
– *Vākyapadīya* I.123

Every cognition in this world is associated with *śabda* and nothing is omitted from the light of *śabda*. Therefore, the intuitive knowledge *pratibhā* and the instincts are all deeply rooted in *śabda* (word). This clearly indicates the all-pervasiveness of Bhartṛhari's language theory which intrudes into the deeper levels of human thoughts.

Pratibhā: Its Sources

To Bhartṛhari, *pratibhā* is *anirvacanīya* (that cannot be described) to others as "it is this". But he tries to explain the ways through which *pratibhā* is manifested. Though the very concept is peculiar to his theory of sentence-meaning, Bhartṛhari uses the word in a broad general perspective, which can be manifested in six different ways and thereby he admits six kinds of intuitions (*pratibhā*). The six sources of *pratibhā* are *svabhāva*, *caraṇa*, *abhyāsa*, *yoga*, *adṛṣṭa* and *viśiṣṭopahita*:

svabhāvacaraṇābhyāsayogādṛṣṭopapāditām |
viśiṣṭopahitāṁ ceti pratibhāṁ ṣaṇvidhāṁ viduḥ ||
– *Vākyapadīya* II.152

Bhartṛhari does not give elucidation and examples for each kind of *pratibhā*, while some explanations are seen in the *Vṛtti* and the commentary of Puṇyarāja. Both these commentaries differ at some points in giving examples of six kinds:

1. The first kind of *pratibhā* is caused by *svabhāva* (nature). The word *svabhāva* refers to the instinctive knowledge of animals, which enables them to engage in activities appropriate to their species. Puṇyarāja illustrates this with an example of monkey and its activities (*Vākyapadīya* II.152). A slightly different opinion is described in the ancient commentary, the *Vṛtti* of

Vākyapadīya. It mentions an example of natural tendency of *prakṛti* (primordial matter) to evolve into *mahat* and our natural tendency of waking up from deep sleep (*Vākyapadīya* II.152).

2. The second cause of *pratibhā* is *caraṇa*, which generally denotes a Vedic school. But here, it signifies *śiṣṭācāra*. This kind of *pratibhā* is awakened, if one strictly follows the duties (*karma*) according to his Vedic school. Puṇyarāja gives no more explanations except for the first kind, saying that all the others are clear and they need no elucidations (*caraṇādiṣūdāharaṇānyūhyāni* – *Vākyapadīya* II.152). The knowledge of the great seer Vasiṣṭha, who acquired special illumination by strictly observing the prescription of his Vedic school, is the example given in the *Vṛtti*:

   caraṇanimittā kācit pratibhā । *tadyathā – ācaraṇenaivāvadhṛtaprakāśaviśeṣāṇāṁ vasiṣṭhādīnām* ॥

   – *Vākyapadīya* II.152

   Raghunatha Sarma also explains the special illumination of Vasiṣṭha through which he could know the events in past, present and future. It indicates that through such observance, one may achieve a spiritual power resulting in a special capacity to perceive things that others are not able to know.

3. The third cause of intuition is *abhyāsa*, which is generally translated as repeated practice. The declarations of expert hydrogeologists and jewellers are prominent examples. Here, the *Vṛtti* suggests an example of the knowledge of a man, who can tell the existence of water for digging a well. All are not able to say where is the suitable place for digging a well, so also the knowledge of the genuineness of precious stones. This knowledge is not identical with inferential knowledge. According to Bhartṛhari, knowledge of genuineness cannot be identified with inferential knowledge

for it requires long practice which enables them to attain that skill. All such knowledge tends to reach a higher stage by practice. The expert knowledge of precious stones and metals is *asamākhyeya* (inexplicable) to others and is caused by *abhyāsa* (regular practice) only. It cannot be achieved by means of *anumāna*. Such an expertise is inherited from a long cultural tradition. This intuition is the result of *āgama* (tradition) accompanied by *bhāvanā*, the tendency to act according to the nature of the different classes of beings. If one gets some instances of referring a particular word with a particular applied meaning due to *abhyāsa*, that word starts indicating that particular meaning, at least for that individual. Thus, *abhyāsa* is also one of the causes of *pratibhā*.

4. *Yoga* is another cause of *pratibhā*. Through *yoga*, one can imagine what is going on in others' mind. The self-consciousness, which is all consciousness, is *pratibhā* and in the light of which, all things are revealed simultaneously and in all their aspects (Kaviraj 1924: 11). The vision of Vasiṣṭha about the real nature of Rāma can be treated as an example for this kind of *pratibhā*. Unable to see Rāma wearing *valkala*, while getting ready to go for forest, Vasiṣṭha closed his eyes for a while. In the meantime he could see the real nature of Rāma (Prasad 2010: 60).

5. The fifth cause of *pratibhā* is *adṛṣṭa*. It is the power of *rākṣasa*s (demons) and *piśāca* (evil spirit) which enables them to enter the bodies of others and make themselves invisible (*Vākyapadīya* II.152, comm. *Vṛtti*). An individual is able to perform some unique activities led by some potency which he requires from his past *karma*. This invisible power is *adṛṣṭa* and due to this power, one can perform supersensible things.

6. Lastly, *pratibhā* is manifested due to *viśiṣṭopahita* (grace of special person). The example illustrated in the *Vṛtti* is the special knowledge which Kṛṣṇadvaipāyana gave to Sañjaya and others; thereby they could see the Kurukṣetra War as such. Again, Lord Kṛṣṇa gives the mystic insight to Arjuna to see his cosmic form in the same context.

Thus it is very clear that *pratibhā* has been conceived in a very comprehensive way in the *Vākyapadīya*. *Pratibhā* exists in every living being accompanied by *bhāvanā*. The manifestations of *pratibhā* range from the basic instincts of animals and birds to the superhuman perceptions of *ṛṣi*s (*ṛṣīṇāmapi yajjñānaṁ tadapyāgamapūrvakam* – *Vākyapadīya* I.30). Thus, we can conclude that the genius of a poet or a scientist or a *ṛṣi* has no quantitative difference from the average man's intuition or instincts of animals.

The Concept of Pratibhā and Its Implications

PRATIBHĀ AND VĀK

The whole second canto of *Vākyapadīya* highlights the semantic nature of *pratibhā*, which has been discussed in detail. But Bhartṛhari treated the concept beyond its linguistic characteristics. He revealed the philosophic as well as psychological outlook of this concept. Bhartṛhari explains the process of cognizing the meaning in a language act in two perspectives. He analyses the speech act both from the points of view of the speaker and the hearer. To him, a linguistic communication can be said complete when the speaker expresses his intention through sounds and the hearer understands what the speaker intends to mean. In this context, what K.A.S. Iyer remarks, is relevant. He puts forth the view that Bhartṛhari perceives *pratibhā* from two different dimensions, i.e. from the point of view of the speaker's experience before utterance and that of the hearer's experience after hearing the utterance. When *pratibhā* is analysed from the hearer's point of view, it is a linguistic entity, which gives rise to the cognition of the sentence-meaning. *Pratibhā* transforms the sentence heard into meaning. This explains the semantic feature of *pratibhā*, where the sentence-meaning shines forth as a flash. When it is analysed from the speaker's angle, *pratibhā* precedes the utterance. Here, *pratibhā* is not conceived in the form of any language and thus the units of language, either in the form of sentence or words, are not important. Coward identifies this state of *pratibhā* with the *paśyantī* stage of *vāk*, after which, comes the utterance (1980: 14-15). The *Vṛtti* also points to this aspect of *pratibhā* (*Vākyapadīya* I.14).

According to Bhartṛhari, the speech principle *vāk* has three stages in the course of its manifestation, viz. *paśyantī*, *madhyamā* and *vaikharī* (*Vākyapadīya* I.144, citation). Later grammarians like Nāgeśa and Kauṇḍabhaṭṭa add another division known as *parā* to this list. This fourfold classification of speech principle is developed in Tantraśāstra and the Pratyabhijñā school of philosophy. According to Bhartṛhari, *parā* and *paśyantī* are identical. Gaurinath Sastri argues that Bhartṛhari accepts no stage higher than *paśyantī* (see Sastri 1959: chaps 1-4). Among these three stages, *vaikharī* form of speech is the first level of speech act, which is called as *dhvani*. This is the physical sound that which is really heard by the sense of hearing and can be differentiated as phonemes, words and sentences. This word is sequential in nature and all the peculiarities of speaker are also present in this state. As the name indicates, *madhyamā* form of speech is an "intermediate" as it lies in between *vaikharī* and *paśyantī*. The language and the thought conveyed by it are undifferentiated in this state. Bhartṛhari says that it is located in the *buddhi* and is accompanied by *prāṇa* (breath). Thus it is psychological in its nature and can be comprehended by the intellect (*Vākyapadīya* I.144). This corresponds to *prākṛta-dhvani* described in the first chapter of *Vākyapadīya*. The third and supreme stage *paśyantī* is the *śabda-brahman*, which is explicated in the opening verse of *Vākyapadīya*. This purest as well as subtlest form of *śabda* is abstract in nature and has no sequence. It is indivisible and beyond worldly use. This has been identified with *pratibhā*, the flash of insight. Vṛṣabhadeva expounds this form of *vāk* in his *Paddhati*, an ancient commentary of *Vākyapadīya*, which reads:

> *pratibhām iti-yeyaṁ samastaśabdārthakāraṇabhūtā buddiḥ, yaṁ paśyantītyāhuḥ, yataḥ śabdāḥ prāṇavṛttim anupatanti, tam anuparā iti anugacchati* ׀ – *Vākyapadīya* I.14

If one tempts to realize this stage of speech, he passes through various stages and ultimately arrives at an undifferentiated state known as *pratibhā*. In this regard Kunjunni Raja observes:

> The complete utterance or the *vākya-sphoṭa* indicates this principle of consciousness, *paśyantī* or *pratibhā*. There is no real distinction between speech and thought at this stage.
> – 1963: 147-48

PRATIBHĀ AND THE SENTENCE-SPHOṬA

As discussed, Bhartṛhari's whole theory of language is firmly rooted in three basic concepts of language, viz. *dhvani*, *sphoṭa* and *pratibhā*. These are three different levels of language, which are interconnected to complete a language act. Among the definitions of sentence mentioned in the *Vākyapadīya*, Bhartṛhari gives emphasis to the definitions held by those, who believe in the indivisibility theory of the sentence. In their perspective, sentence is defined as sentence-*sphoṭa*, and sentence-meaning is *pratibhā*. Thus, it is clear that sentence-*sphoṭa* and sentence-meaning *pratibhā* are two distinct concepts coined by Bhartṛhari. *Sphoṭa* can be taken as an auditory impression manifested by articulated sounds (*dhvani*) whereas *pratibhā* refers to the meaning conveyed by the sentence. Meaning is understood only after the auditory perception of sound. Therefore, *pratibhā* is aroused only after the *sphoṭa* is manifested.

Different opinions are held by scholars in this regard. Scholars like J. Brough, Kunjunni Raja and K.A.S. Iyer argue that *sphoṭa* is the linguistic sign in its aspect of meaning-bearer. According to them, *sphoṭa* is not a mystic entity as suggested by A.B. Keith (1928: 387), but they consider the *sphoṭa* doctrine as the theory of language symbolism. This concept of *sphoṭa* explains the problem of how language is grasped in a verbal communication. But the problem of meaning of the sentence is yet to be unravelled. They maintain that *sphoṭa* in general and sentence-*sphoṭa* in particular has been assumed as a solution to this problem. On the contrary they opine that *pratibhā* as a flash of understanding is the sentence-meaning. These two arguments are self-contradictory. Here what Matilal remarks seems to be more agreeable. To quote him:

> For Bhartṛhari, however, this is a wrong term: "meaning-bearing unit". *Sphoṭa* is the real substratum, proper linguistic unit, which is identical also with its meaning. Language is not the vehicle of meaning or the conveyor-belt of thought. Thought anchors language and language anchors thought. *Śabdanā* (languaging), is thinking; and thought vibrates through language. In this way of looking at things, there cannot be any essential difference between a linguistic unit and its meaning or the thought it conveys. *Sphoṭa* refers to this non-differentiated language-principle. Thus I believe that it is sometimes even incorrect to ask whether *sphoṭa* is or is not the meaning-bearing speech unit in Bhartṛhari's system.
>
> – 1992: 85

If the *sphoṭa* theory arose as a solution to the problem of understanding language, Bhartṛhari would not have introduced the concept of *pratibhā* as sentence-meaning. Thus, it can be comprehended that Bhartṛhari puts forth the concept of sentence-*sphoṭa*, which explains the language principle so as to how language is used and grasped. While, the concept of *pratibhā* is introduced to solve the problem of how language is understood (Rath 2000: 164-65). The auditory impressions are transformed into meaning in the mind by the virtue of *pratibhā*.

PRATIBHĀ AND THE CONCEPT OF TRANSFORMATIONS IN MODERN LINGUISTICS

Recent researches in the field of syntax and semantics have presented various theories regarding the analysis of sentence. The psycho-linguistic approaches of transformational linguistics[3] revolutionanized the scientific study of sentence and its meaning. The two major prospects of transformational grammar are "linguistic competency" and "generative grammar". These two concepts are developed by the later cognitive linguists such as Noam Chomsky (1957) and Ronald Langacker (1987). In contrast with the structuralists, transformational linguists believe that the proper object of linguistic study is the knowledge that the native speaker possesses, which enables them to produce and understand various sentences. This knowledge is termed as "competence". According to Chomsky, this is innate and he called it as "innate linguistic knowledge" or "innate language competency". The concept of

---

[3] The linguist's approach towards the analysis of a sentence is mainly of four types: traditional; comparative and historical; structural and descriptive; and transformational. The traditional grammarians break up the word order to analyse the relationship between the words such as nouns and adjectives. On the other side, linguists like Otto Jespersen tried to analyse language in a historical and comparative methodology. They hold that language undergoes constant change and thus the prototypes can be traced through the historical and comparative analysis. As scholars focused more on language and less on history, they introduced a new methodology in analysing language. These scholars approach language in two ways, synchronic and diachronic, which focus on the structural analysis of language. This methodology has been developed by a group of linguists called structuralists. The goals, methods and assumptions of transformational grammarians are unique and different from those of descriptive linguistics. In contrast with the structuralists, they consider grammar to be a system of rules that generate exactly those combinations of words which form grammatical sentences in a given language. They developed the concept of "transformations" which helps the user to produce new sentences from the existing ones.

generative grammar tries to define rules that can generate the infinite number of grammatical sentence possible in a language. This method of grammar uses the concept of "transformations" which helps people to produce new sentences from the existing ones. To explain this concept, Chomsky sets forth the idea that each sentence in a language has two levels of representation; a deep structure and a surface structure. The deep structure represents the core semantic relations of a sentence and is mapped on to the surface structure via transformations. Thus, deep structures can be perceived as a universal grammar underlying the language act and corresponding to the linguistic competence.

On a shrewd analysis of the concept of *pratibhā*, conceived by Bhartṛhari, it can be stated that *pratibhā* is the prototype of "transformations". In a conversation, the listener first grasps the speech in terms of words, one after the other. This manifests the internal *sphoṭa* (*buddhistha-śabda*), which is the auditory impression of the uttered speech. At this level it resembles the concept of "deep structure" presented by the transformationalists. Sudden after the manifestation of the internal *sphoṭa*, *pratibhā*, the intuitive instinct transforms it into the meaning. Similar process is adopted by the cognitive linguists, when they explain that the deep structure is mapped on to the surface structure via transformations.

It has been a topic of debate among the scholars of linguistics as well as psychology that how a child acquires his/her first language. Some of them accept the role of instinct as not so useful in the child's language acquisition, while some others hold the view that child's language is a product of instinct (Rath 2000: 151-52). Chomsky answers this vexed problem by his notions of generative grammar and innate linguistic knowledge. In his cognitive theory, Chomsky suggests that language acquisition is based on various rules and regulations. A child, who comes in contact with various language features, makes his/her own rules though unconsciously. Earlier, it was believed that the children grasp their preliminary words from either their parents or other elders.

But recent linguistic trends do not accept that parents "teach" children their first language. The reason is no parent has the necessary explicit knowledge to do so, and children anyway acquire the knowledge of their first language long before they are in a position to understand the relevant instructions of their parents (Smith 2004: 116). In his theory of "cognitive capability", Chomsky argues that people possess a kind of language faculty which is a part of human natural biological qualities. This idea is known as "innate language faculty", which has a basic grammar system which is termed as "universal grammar" (Jyothirmayi 2009: 283). This innate linguistic knowledge enables a child to acquire the notion of structure, which helps the child to learn any language.

Bhartr̥hari also holds similar view with Chomsky and he emphasizes on the role of intuition in child's language acquisition. He opines that it is *śabda-bhāvanā* that enables a newborn baby to make the first movements of vocal organs. Stimulated by this *śabda-bhāvanā*, air coming out of baby's mouth is able to strike at certain points of articulation and produce sounds. The *Vr̥tti* again mentions that there is no other reason than *pratibhā* to make these movements.

ādyaḥ karaṇavinyāsaḥ prāṇasyordhnaṁ samīraṇam ।
sthānānāmabhighātaśca na vinā śabdabhāvanām ॥
– *Vākyapadīya* I.122

This theory of word-impregnatedness of Bhartr̥hari is akin to the innate language competency of the transformationalists. Even though Chomsky's concepts of language are different from that of Bhartr̥hari, there are resemblences between *pratibhā* and Chomsky's "innate language faculty". Both are innate and instinctive in nature and explain the process through which children gain the knowledge of language.

In Indian scenario, Mīmāṁsakas and Naiyāyikas also present a similar concept in the child's language acquisition, with slight changes. They also state that children first understand the sentence as a whole and later, by the process of inclusion and exclusion (*āvāpa* and *udvāpa*), they come to know about the individual meanings of the words. Gradually, they are able to understand and produce new sentences. The process is elaborated in the *Nyāyasiddhāntamuktāvalī* as:

> *evam vyavahārādapi yathā prayojakavṛddhena ghaṭa-mānayetyuktaṁ tacchrutvā prayojyavṛddhena ghaṭa ānītastadavadhārya pārśvastho bālo ghaṭānayanarūpakāryaṁ ghaṭamānayeti śabdaprayojyamityavadhārayati। tataśca ghaṭaṁ naya gāṁ badhānetyādivākyād āvāpodvāpābhyaṁ ghaṭādipadānāṁ kāryānvitaghaṭādau śaktiṁ gṛhṇāti ... prathamataḥ kāryānvitaghaṭādau śaktyavadhāraṇe 'pi lāghavena paścāttasya parityāgaucityāt।* – *Kārikāvalī* 1988: 561-63

The sum total of this discussion is that Bhartṛhari was the first to introduce the instinctive innate knowledge of a person called *pratibhā* into the realm of linguistics. This innate capacity enables a person to understand and produce various sentences and is manifested by the indivisible sentence-*sphoṭa*. The concept of transformations introduced by the modern cognitive linguists is akin to Bhartṛhari's *pratibhā* in several aspects.

5

Conclusion

LANGUAGE is generally perceived as the medium for communicating one's ideas to the other. Thus, language faculty includes not mere linguistic factors, but psychological as well as social factors are also significant. This communication or transference of thought takes place through meaningful linguistic units and each meaningful unit represents a complete thought. This meaningful linguistic unit is in the form of sentence and, thus, linguists and grammarians accept sentence as the unit of communication. Therefore, the study of sentence and sentence-meaning has drawn the serious attention of linguists, grammarians and philosophers. The ancient scholars in India called this meaningful linguistic unit as *śabda* and it was accepted as one of the means of valid knowledge (*śabda-pramāṇa*). As a result of this serious attention given to the concept of sentence by the Eastern scholars, various theories and concepts have evolved in the realm of language studies.

In the present study titled *The Concept of Sentence and Meaning: Vistas in Indian Milieu*, emphasis has been given to the various propositions of the concept of sentence and sentence-meaning. Here, a humble attempt is made to understand the ways in which these concepts are envisaged in the different systems of thought in India. While going through the detailed discussions on the perspectives of different thinkers on these concepts, the following observations are made:

1. Almost all schools of thought accept *śabda* as a distinct means of valid knowledge as it unveils the knowledge hitherto unknown. The term *śabda* is used to denote the meaningful linguistic unit and it is generally defined as in the form of sentence.
2. The concept of sentence is defined in manifold ways by the preceptors of different schools of thought. In general, the sentence is defined in two perspectives: Sakhaṇḍa and Akhaṇḍa. The former school treat sentence as a collection of semantically connected words. Though sentence is an aggregation of its parts, it denotes a unified sense and, thus, is considered as a unified entity, which is distinct from the parts. The factors that constitute the unity of sentence are *ākāṅkṣā*, *yogyatā* and *sannidhi*. The individual words in the sentence are interconnected by these factors. Sanskriticians give emphasis to these factors in their discussions on the concept of sentence. On the other side, a group of philosophers hold that sentence is an indivisible unit of language (*eko 'navayavaḥ śabdaḥ*), devoid of any parts. This is the Akhaṇḍa school of sentence.
3. If sentence is defined as the aggregation of words, the meaning of sentence is also decided by the meanings of the individual words. The individual words are associated semantically to denote a unified sense. This particular meaning is distinct from the meanings of the parts. This process of the cognition of sentence-meaning, derived from the semantic association of words, is generally termed as *śābdabodha* (verbal cognition).
4. There are two subdivisions under *śābdabodha,* viz. *khaṇḍa-śābdabodha* and *akhaṇḍa-śābdabodha*. In the first variety,

the import is produced by the parts of the sentence while in the latter, it is produced as a unitary whole. Almost all Indian thinkers are in fond of *khaṇḍa-pakṣa* of verbal import, while Bhartṛhari and his followers set forth the theory of *akhaṇḍa-śābdabodha*.

5. There are two major theories in the *khaṇḍa-pakṣa* of verbal import, viz. Abhihitānvayavāda and Anvitābhidhānavāda. The followers of the Bhāṭṭa school of Mīmāṁsā and a group of Naiyāyikas are the major followers of the *abhihitānvaya* theory. The essence of this theory is that the words in a sentence first designate their meanings and then the word-meanings are brought together to give the sentence-meaning. While Prabhākara, the founder of the Prābhākara school of Mīmāṁsā, and his followers believe in the latter theory of verbal import. According to them, each word in the sentence gives a connected meaning and hence the meaning of the sentence can be comprehended from each word.
6. Bhartṛhari, who upholds the theory of indivisibility of sentence and sentence-meaning, accepts *akhaṇḍa-vākyasphoṭa* as the real nature of sentence and *pratibhā*, a flash of understanding, as the sentence-meaning. These concepts are elaborately discussed in the Vākyakāṇḍa of *Vākyapadīya*.
7. Bhartṛhari examines language in three levels, viz. analytic level, communicative level and ultimate level. As a method of communication, language is the carrier of thoughts and thoughts cannot be communicated in bits and pieces. Thus, sentence is the unit of communicating ideas and it is also indivisible in nature.
8. Bhartṛhari is a staunch believer of the indivisibility theory of sentence and sentence-meaning and he provides a number of arguments to support this theory. Just like the perception of

a multicoloured picture, which is evolved as a unity in spite of subsequent analysis into its component coloured parts, a cognition presenting different jobs as its contents is a unitary entity in reality (*Vākyapadīya* II.8-9). It is indivisible into several individual cognitions. Though a sentence has various components in subsequent analysis, it is cognized as unitary whole by the speaker as well as the listener. If a sentence is divisible into words and words into phonemes, then this division has to be carried out further. Therefore, the sentence is accepted as undivided into constituent parts and conveys one single meaning.

9. The individuality of the subsequent words in the sentence is also explained by Bhartṛhari in the analytic level of language. For the purpose of grammar, sentence can be analysed into its parts such as noun, verb, etc. This is not real, but is carried out in the mind. Bhartṛhari termed this unique concept as *apoddhāra*. Though the listener grasps the sentence as the sequence of words, the sudden flash of understanding *pratibhā*, cognizes the meaning of the sentence as a whole. After the cognition of sentence-meaning, he identifies the individual words and their meanings by the process *apoddhāra*.
10. While discussing about the meaning of the sentence, Bhartṛhari introduces the theory of *pratibhā*, which states that the sentence conveys its meaning in a flash. To explain how sentence is comprehended, Bhartṛhari goes beyond the level of uttered speech. In order to explain the problem of linguistic communications, he introduces this very concept, which signifies the intuitive linguistic disposition. From both the point of views of the speaker and the listener, the sentence-meaning cannot be accepted as that which is built up gradually on the basis of word-meanings. It is

grasped through an instantaneous flash of insight. This instantaneous understanding is neither spatial, nor particular, nor dependent on the peculiarities of a particular language. It is the instinctive power of the mind. Thus, *pratibhā* can be experienced, but cannot be expressed to others in terms of "it is this".

11. Bhartṛhari expounds the important characteristics of *pratibhā* in several verses. From the listener's point of view, *pratibhā* is the meaning of a sentence and thus, it is the semantic unit of language. But Bhartṛhari also explores the deeper levels of this concept. From the speaker's point of view, it is identical with the *paśyantī* state of *vāk*. This unravels the psychological as well as the philosophical outlook of *pratibhā*.
12. Bhartṛhari explains six kinds of *pratibhā* and, thus, is conceived in a very comprehensive way. The manifestations of *pratibhā* range from the basic instincts of animals and birds to the superhuman perceptions of *ṛṣis*. Thus, the concept of *pratibhā*, introduced by Bhartṛhari goes beyond the level of communicating the sentence-meaning. He conceives it as an intuitive instinct, the implications of which, can better explain several philosophical and psychological aspects of human language and thoughts.
13. But this innovative way of thinking introduced by Bhartṛhari was not developed by the later scholars over the centuries. Later in modern linguistics, structuralism and behaviourism tried to analyse only language performance. They overlooked the idea of language competence and the cognitive grammar of language. The transformational or cognitive way of thought developed by Bhartṛhari remains stagnated till the second half of twentieth century. It was in 1970s that scholars like Charles Fillmore (1993), George Lakoff (1977), Ronald Langacker

(1987) and Leonard Talmy (1978), who did not follow the prevailing tendency to explain linguistic patterns by means of appeals to structural properties internal to and specific to language, tried to rediscover the cognitive principles of language. Later, the basic concepts of Chomskian school of linguistics tried to bring back a rich tradition of generative grammar and cognitive philosophy of language. It was Noam Chomsky, who tried to identify the theories behind language competence and put forth unique and innovative theories regarding the relation of language and mind. Thus modern linguists tried to develop the innovative ideas of Bhartṛhari and explore new horizons in the field of linguistics and psychology.

14. Recent trends in linguistics point to the necessity of deconstructing the views of Bhartṛhari in the light of the revolutionary concepts of Modern Transformational Linguists. The major theories of transformationalists are "generative grammar" and "language competency". These theories resemble Bhartṛhari's concepts of sentence and sentence-meaning in manifold ways.

Modern linguistics has become a fast developing area of study encompassing various other fields of learning such as psychology, sociology, philosophy, cognitive sciences and Information Technology. Linguists have different opinions on vexed questions like what is a sentence? What constitutes the sentence-meaning? How is a sentence constituted? How is the meaning of a sentence cognized as a whole by the listener? These problems have emerged into the realm of semantics very recently. Transformational linguists and cognitive linguists contributed much in the field of syntax and semantics. The revolutionary ideas of modern cognitive linguists such as Chomsky and Langacker were erected upon the studies of the concept of sentence and cognition of the sentence-meaning.

In the light of these revolutionary developments of transformational and cognitive linguistics, the so-called "mystic" ideas of Bhartṛhari on sentence and sentence-meaning can be deconstructed. The concept of sentence as a unitary whole and *pratibhā*, an intuitive instinct as the meaning of sentence can be analysed beyond its linguistic characteristics. The psycho-linguistic analysis of the concept of *pratibhā*, in the light of modern cognitive linguistics, has a wide scope to study further. In addition to this, Bhartṛhari states that the sentence-meaning is a flash of awareness, which happens in memory (*smṛti*). This aspect of *pratibhā* can also be taken up for further study connecting neuroscience and psycho-linguistics. Thus, it can be concluded with the remarks of Jan Houben:

> Modern cognitive linguists and construction grammarians, on their part, may find to their surprise an extensive amount of investigations in Bhartṛhari's work and in the Bhartṛharian way of Pāṇinian grammar that directly pertain to basic issues in their research programme. A rapprochement between Bhartṛhari studies and cognitive linguistics is therefore expected to be most fruitful and stimulating for both parties. – 2009: 539

Many modern scholars are endeavouring in this area of studies, but Bhartṛhari and his *Vākyapadīya* still remain the sources of endless innovative and scholarly speculations even in this era.

Bibliography

Primary Sources

Amarakośa of Amarasiṁha, with the unpublished south Indian comm. *Amarapadavivṛti* of Liṅgāyasūrin, *Amarapadapārijāta* of Mallīnātha and *Amarapadavivaraṇa* of Appayārya, ed. A.A. Ramanathan, Madras: Adyar Library and Research Centre, 1983.

Aṣṭādhyāyī of Pāṇini, ed. Gopal Dutt Pandey, Varanasi: Chaukhamba Surabharati Prakashan, 2016.

Brahmasūtra with *Śāṅkarabhāṣyam*, Varanasi: Chowkhamba Vaidyabhavan, 1962.

Bṛhaddevatā of Śaunaka, ed. Arthur Anthony Macdonell, Delhi: Motilal Banarsidass, 1965.

Bṛhatī of Prabhākaramiśra, with the comm. *Ṛjuvimalapañcikā* of Śālikanātha, ed. S. Subrahmanya Sastri, Madras: University of Madras, 1967.

Dhvanyāloka of Ānandavardhana, with the comm. *Locana* of Abhinavagupta, Varanasi: Chowkhamba Vidyabhavan, 2006.

Gaṇaratnamahodadhi of Vardhamāna, with the *Vṛtti*, ed. Julius Eggeling, Delhi: Motilal Banarsidass, 1963.

Jaiminipraṇītaṁ Mīmāṁsādarśanam, with the *Bhāṣya* of Śabara, Poona: Anandasram Sanskrit Series, 1972.

Kārikāvalī of Viśvanāthapañcānana, along with *Siddhāntamuktāvalī* and comm., *Prabhā, Mañjūṣā, Dinakarī, Rāmarudrī* and *Gaṅgārāmī*, ed. C. Shankar Ram Shastri, Delhi: Chaukhamba Sanskrit Pratishthan, 1988.

Kāśhikāvṛitti of Vāmana and Jayādityā, 1985, ed. Narayana Mishra Varanasi: Ratna Pubicatiions.

Kāvyādarśa of Daṇḍin, with the comm. *Prakāśa*, ed. Ramachandra Misra, Varanasi: Chowkhamba Vidya Bhavan, 2005.

Kāvyālaṁkāra of Bhāmaha, ed. Nagnath Shastry, Delhi: Motilal Banarsidass, 1966.

Kāvyālāṁkārasūtravṛtti of Vāmana, ed. Kedarnath Sharma, Delhi: Chaukhamba Sanskrit Series, 1979.

Kāvyaprakāśa of Mammaṭa, with the comm. *Bālabodhinī* of Bhaṭṭavāmana, Pune: Bhandarkar Oriental Research Institute, 1983.

Mahābhāṣya of Patañjali (Navāhnikam), with the comm. *Pradīpa* of Kaiyaṭa, *Udyota* of Nāgeśa and *Tattvāloka* of Rudradhara Jha, Varanasi: Chaukhamba Sanskrit Sansthan, 1984.

Mahābhāṣya of Patañjali, with the comm., *Bhāṣyapradīpa* of Kaiyaṭa and *Udyota* of Nāgeśa, 6 vols, Delhi: Chaukhamba Sanskrit Series, 1991.

Mānameyodaya of Nārāyaṇa, Madras: Adyar Library and Research Centre, 1975.

Mānameyodaya of Nārāyaṇa, Varanasi: Chaukhamba Vidya Bhavan, 1996.

Mīmāṁsādarśanam of Jaimini, along with *Śabarabhāṣya* of Śabaramuni *Bhāṣyavivaraṇa* of Govindamuni, *Tantravārtika* of Kumārila and *Nyāyasudhā* of Bhaṭṭasomeśvara, ed. Mahaprabhu Lal Gosvami, Varanasi: Tara Printing Works, 1984.

Nirukta of Yāska, with the comm. of Durgācārya, ed. M.M. Pandit Mukund Jha Bakshi, Delhi: Chaukhamba Sanskrit Pratishthan, 2002.

Nyāyadarśanam of Gautama, with the *Nyāyabhāṣya* of Vātsyāyana, *Vārtika* of Udyotakara, *Ṭīkā* of Vācaspatimiśra and the comm. *Pariśuddhi* of Udayana (chap. 1), ed. Ananth Lal Thakur, Darbhanga: Mithila Institute Series, 1967.

Nyāyakośa or Dictionary of Technical Terms of Indian Philosophy by Maha Mahopadhyaya Bhimacharya Jhalakikah, Poone: Bhandarkar Oriental Research Institute, 1928.

Nyāyakusumāñjali of Udayana, with the comm. *Kusumāñjalivistāra*, Tirupati: Rashtriya Sanskrit Vidyapeetha, 1980.

Nyāyamañjarī of Jayantabhaṭṭa, with the comm. *Nyāyasaurabhai,* ed. K.S. Varadacharya, Mysore: Oriental Research Institute, 1970.

Nyāyasudhā of Jayatīrtha, with six comm., Bangalore: Madhvasidhantabhivrdhikarinisabha, 1982.

Paramalaghumañjūṣā of Nāgeśabhaṭṭa, with the comm. *Bhāvaprakāśikā* and *Bālabodhinī* by Jayashankar Lal Tripathi, Varanasi: Krishnadas Academy, 1985.

Pātañjalayogasūtraṇī, with *Vyāsabhāṣya* and comm. by Vācaspati Miśra, ed. Hari Narayan Apte, Ananda Ashram Press, Pune, 1904.

Pātañjalayogadarśanam of Patañjali, with the comm. of Vyāsa, Varanasi: Chaukhamba Sanskrit Series, 1970.

Prakaraṇapañcikā of Śālikanātha, with the comm. of Jayapura Nārāyaṇa Bhaṭṭa, ed. A. Subramanya Sastri, Varanasi: Banares Hindu University, 1961.

Prakaraṇapañcikā of Śālikanātha, with an exposition in English, ed. and tr. K.T. Pandurangi, New Delhi: Indian Council of Philosophical Research and D.K. Printworld, 2004.

Rājataraṅgiṇī of Kalhaṇa, tr. M.A. Stein, Delhi: Motilal Banarsidass, 2009.

Ṛgveda, with the *Padapāṭha* and the available portions of the *Bhāṣyas* by Skandasvāmin and Udgītha, the *Vyākhyā* by Veṅkaṭa-Mādhava and Mudgala's Vṛtti Based on Sāyaṇabhāṣya, part III, ed. Vishva Bandhu, Hoshiarpur: Vishveshvaranand Vedic Research Institute, 1963.

Ṛgvedaprātiśākhyam of Śaunaka, with the comm. of *Uvvaṭācārya,* ed. Rāmaprasāda Tripāṭhī, Varanasi: Sampurnanand Sanskrit Vishvavidyalaya, 1986.

Śabdakaustubha of Bhaṭṭojidīkṣita, with Jayakṛṣṇa's *Sphoṭacandrikā*, ed. Vindhyesvari Prasada Dvivedin, Ganapati Sastri Mokate, Varanasi: Chaukhamba Sanskrit Sansthan, 1933.

Śabdaśaktiprakāśikā of Jagadīśa, with the comm. *Kṛṣṇakāntī* of Kṛṣṇakāntavidyāvāgīśa and *Prabodhinī* of Rāmabhadrasiddhāntavāgīśa, ed. Ḍhuṇḍhirājaśāstrī, Varanasi: Chowkhamba Sanskrit Series Office, 2002.

Sāṁkhyasūtras of Kapila, along with the *Bhāṣya* of Vijñānabhikṣu, ed. Ram Shankar Bhattacharya, Varanasi: Bharatiya Vidya Prakashan, 1966.

Sarvadarśanasaṁgraha of Mādhava, tr. E.B. Cowell and A.E. Gough, ed. K.L. Joshi, Delhi: Parimal Publications, 1981.

Śatapatha Brāhmaṇa, with *Ratna-dīpikā,* Hindi tr. Pt. Gaṅgā Prasād Upādhyāya, vols I-III, New Delhi: The Research Institute of Ancient Scientific Studies, 1970.

Ślokavārtika of Kumārilabhaṭṭa, with the comm. *Nyāyaratnākara* of Pārthasārathimiśra, Benares: Chowkhamba Sanskrit Series Office, 1898.

Ślokavārtika of Kumārilabhaṭṭa, with the comm. *Kāśikā* and *Nyāyaratnākara* of Pārthasārathimiśra, tr. G.N. Jha, Delhi: Sri Satguru Publications, 1983.

Ślokavārtika of Kumārilabhaṭṭa, tr. Ganganatha Jha, Calcutta: Asiatic Society, 1985.

Ślokavārtika of Kumārilabhaṭṭa, 1990, with the comm. *Kāśikā*, ed. K. Sambasivasastri, Trivandrum: Trivandrum Sanskrit Series, 1990.

Sphoṭasiddhi of Maṇḍana Miśra, ed. and tr. K.A. Subramania Iyer, Poona: Deccan College, 1966.

Sphoṭavāda of Nāgeśabhaṭṭa, ed. with comm. *Subodhinī* by V. Kṛṣṇamācārya, Madras: Adyar Library, 1946.

Taittirīya Saṁhitā, ed. T.M. Narayana Sastri, Kumbhakonam: Sharadavilasa Publications, 1931.

Tantravārtika of Kumārilabhaṭṭa, Aitihāsika Saṅkīrṇa Sāhitya 97, Poona, 1929.

Tarkabhāṣā of Keśavamiśra, with the comm. *Tattvaprabodhinī*, Karnataka: Krishnaprabha Prakashan, 1995.

Tarkakaumudī of Laugākṣibhāskara, ed. M.N. Dvivedi, Benares Sanskrit Series 32, Varanasi, 1886.

Tarkasaṁgraha of Annambhaṭṭa, with the comm. *Tarkadīpikā* and *Nyāyabodhinī*, Delhi: Motilal Banarsidass, 1971.

Tattvabindu of Vācaspatimiśra, with comm. *Tattvabhāvanā* of Parameśvara, Annamalai Sanskrit Series 3, Annamalai, 1936.

Tattvacintāmaṇi of Gaṅgeśa, ed. Kāmākhyānātha, vol. 4, Delhi: Chaukhamba Sanskrit Sansthan, 1990.

The Vākyapadīya-Brahmakāṇḍam of Bhartṛhari, with the comm. *Prakāśa* by Narain Datt Tripathi, ed. Avadh Bihari Mishra, Benares: Banārasa Siṭī 1937.

The Vākyapadīya: A Treatise on the Philosophy of Sanskrit Grammar by Bhartṛhari, Brahma Kāṇḍa, with the comm. *Bhāvapradīpa* and notes by Suryanārāyaṇa Śukla, Benares: Kasi Sanskrit College, 1937.

The Vyākaraṇa Mahābhāṣya of Patañjali, ed. F. Kielhorn, revised and furnished with additional readings, references and select critical notes by K.V. Abhyankar, Poona: Bhandarkar Oriental Research Institute, 1962.

Vaiyākaraṇabhūṣaṇasāra of Kauṇḍabhaṭṭa, Poona: Anandasrama Press, 1957.

Vākyapadīya of Bhartṛhari, ed. K.V. Abhyankar and V.P. Limaye, Poona: Univesrity of Poona, 1965.

Vākyapadīya of Bhartṛhari, with the comm. *Vṛtti* and *Paddhati* of Vṛṣabhadeva, Kāṇḍa I, ed. K.A. Subramaniya Iyer, Poona: Deccan College, 1966.

Vākyapadīyam, part III (Padakāṇḍa) (Vṛttisamuddeśa), with the comm. *Prakāśa* by Helārāja and *Ambākartrī* by Raghunātha Śarmā, Varanasi: Sampurnanand Sanskrit University, 1977.

Vākyapadīyam, part III (Padakāṇḍa), with the comm. *Prakāśa* by Helārāja and *Ambākartrī* by Raghunātha Śarmā, vol. II, Varanasi: Sampurnanand Sanskrit University, 1979.

Vākyapadīyam, part II (Vākyakāṇḍa), with the comm. *Ambākartrī* by Raghunātha Śarmā, Varanasi: Sampurnanand Sanskrit University, 1980.

Vākyapadīyam, part III (Padakāṇḍa), with the comm. *Prakāśa* by Helārāja and *Ambākartrī* by Raghunātha Śarmā, vol. I, Varanasi: Sampurnanand Sanskrit University, 1991.

Vākyapadīya of Bhartṛhari (Kāṇḍa II), containing the *Ṭīkā* of Puṇyarāja and the Ancient *Vṛtti*, ed. K.A. Subramania Iyer, Delhi: Motilal Banarsidass, 1983.

Vākyapadīya of Bhartṛhari, with comm. of Helārāja, Kāṇḍa III, part I, ed. K.A Subramania Iyer, Poona: Deccan College, 1994.

Vakapadīya-Brahmakānda, of Bhartṛhari with the Comm. Pratyekārthaprakāśikā by M.M. Dravyeśa Jha, New Delhi: Mandākinī Sanskrit-Vidvat Parishad, 2002

Vākyapadīyam, part I (Brahmakāṇḍa), with the comm. *Svopajñavṛtti* by Harivṛṣabha and *Ambākartrī* by Raghunātha Śarmā, Varanasi: Sampurnanand Sanskrit University, 2006.

Vākyapadīyam of Bhartṛhari (Brahmakāṇḍa), with the comm. *Pratibhā* by Vamdev Acharya, ed. Satyanarayan Shastri Khanduri, Varanasi: Chowkhamba Krishnadas Academy, 2007.

Vedāntaparibhāṣā of Dharmarāja Adhvarindra, with the comm. *Maṇiprabhā* of Amaradāsa and *Śikhāmaṇi* of Rāmakṛṣṇādhvarin, ed. Swami Govinda Sinha Sadhu, Mumbai: Venkatesvara Press, 1985.

Vyutpattivāda of Gadādhara, with the comm. *Dīpikā* of Paṇḍita Śivadatta Miśra, ed. Jwala Prasad Gaur, Varanasi: Bharatiya Vidya Prakashan, 1973.

Secondary Sources

ENGLISH WORKS

Aklujkar, Ashok, 1969, "Two Textual Studies of Bhartṛhari", *Journal of the American Oriented Society* 89(3): 547-63.

———, 1972, "The Authorship of the *Vākyapadīya-Vṛtti*", *WZKSOA* 16: 181-98.

———, 1983, "Foreword", in *Vākyapadīya of Bhartṛhari*, Kāṇḍa II, ed. K.A. Subramania Iyer, Delhi: Motilal Banarsidass.

———, 1990, "Introduction and Summary of the First Two Books of the Vākyapadīya" in *The Philosophy of the Grammarians*, ed. Harold G. Coward and K. Kunjunni Raja, Delhi: Motilal Banarsidass.

———, 1991, "Syntactic Gleanings from Bhartṛhari's Trikāṇḍī", in *Studies in Sanskrit Syntax*, ed. Hans Henrich Hock, Delhi: Motilal Banarsidass.

———, 1993, "An Introduction to the Study of Bhartṛhari", in *Bhartṛhari: Philosopher and Grammarian*, ed. Saroja Bhate, Johannes Bronkhorst, Delhi: Motilal Banarsidass.

Banerji, Suresh Chandra, 1996, *Historical Survey of Ancient Indian Grammar,* Delhi: Sharada Publishing House.

Bhate, Saroja and Johannes Bronkhorst (eds), 1993, *Bhartṛhari: Philosopher and Grammarian*, Delhi: Motilal Banarsidass.

Bhatta, V.P., 1991, *Epistemology, Logic and Grammar in the Analysis of Sentence-Meaning,* vol.1, Delhi: Eastern Book Linkers.

Bhattacharyya, Sibajiban, 1984, "Some Indian Theories of Meaning", *The Journal of the Indian Academy of Philosophy*, 23(2): 25-41.

———, (ed.), 2004, *Words and Sentence: Two Perspectives: Bhartṛhari and Wittgenstein,* New Delhi: Sahitya Akademi.

Brett, R.L. and A.R. Jones (eds), 1963, *Lyrical Ballads: William Wordsworth, Samuel Taylor Coleridge*, London: Methun and Co.

Bronkhorst, Johannes, 1994, "Bhartṛhari and Mīmāṁsā" in *Studies in Mīmāṁsā*, ed. R.C. Dwivedi, Delhi: Motilal Banarsidass.

Brough, John, 1951, "Theories of General Linguistics in the Sanskrit Grammarians", in *Transactions of the Philological Society*, pp. 27-46, Oxford: Philological Society..

———, 1953, "Some Indian Theories of Meaning", *Transactions of the Philological Society*, pp. 161-76.

Cardona, George, 1980, *Pāṇini: A Survey of Research*, Delhi: Motilal Banarsidass.

Chatterjee, S.C., 1939, *The Nyāya Theory of Knowledge*, Calcutta: University of Calcutta.

Chaturvedi, Mithilesh, 2001, *Vṛttisamuddeśa of Bhartṛhari's Vākyapadīya: A Study*, Delhi: Shivalik Prakashan.

———, (ed.), 2009, *Bhartṛhari*: *Language, Thought and Reality*, Delhi: Motilal Banarsidass.

Chomsky, Noam, 1957, *Syntactic Structures*, The Hague: Mouton and Co.

———, 1968, *Language and Mind*, New York: Harcourt.

———, 1972, *Studies on Semantics in Generative Grammar*, The Hague: Mouton and Co.

Coward, Harold G., 1976, *Bhartṛhari*, Boston: Twayne Publishers.

———, 1980, *The Sphoṭa Theory of Language*, Delhi: Motilal Banarsidass.

———, 1991, "Derrida and Bhartṛhari's Vākyapadīya on the Origin of Language", in *Derrida and Indian Philosophy*, ed. Harold Coward Delhi: Motilal Banarsidass.

Coward, Harold G. and K. Kunjunni Raja (eds), 2008, *The Philosophy of the Grammarians*, Delhi: Motilal Banarsidass.

Dasgupta, Surendranath, 1975, *A History of Indian Philosophy*, 5 vols, Delhi: Motilal Banarsidass.

de Saussure, F., 1959, *Course in General Linguistics*, tr. Wade Baskin, New York: Columbia University Press.

Fillmore, Charles J. and Paul Kay, 1993, *Construction Grammar Coursebook*, Berkeley: University of California.

Hariharopādhyaya, 1912, Bhartṛhari Nirvedam, ed. Dugraprasada Dvivedi and Vāsūdeva Lakshmana Panashikara Mumbai: Nirnaya Sagar Press.

Hota, A.N., 1985, "Sphoṭa, Pratibhā and Dhvani", Dissertation, Pune: CASS.

Houben, Jan E.M., 1996, "Socio-linguistic Attitudes Reflected in the Work of Bhartṛhari and Later Grammarians", in *Ideology and Status of Sanskrit*, ed. Jan E.M. Houben, Leiden: E.J. Brill.

———, 2009, "Bhartṛhari as a 'Cognitive Linguist'", in *Bhartṛhari*: *Language, Thought and Reality*, ed. Mithilesh Chaturvedi, Delhi: Motilal Banarsidass.

Huxley, Aldous, 2000, *Complete Essays of Aldous Huxley*, vol. 1, ed. Robert S. Baker and James Sexton, Chicago: Ivan R. Dee.

Iyer, K.A. Subramania, 1941, "Pratibhā as the Meaning of Sentence", in Proceedings of the 10th All-India Oriental Conference, Madras.

———, (tr.), 1965, *The Vākyapadīya of Bhartṛhari with the Vṛtti*, Chapter I, Poona: Deccan College.

———, (tr.), 1969, *Bhartṛhari: A Study of the Vākyapadīya in the Light of the Ancient Commentaries*, Poona: Deccan College.

———, (tr.), 1971, The *Vākyapadīya of Bhartṛhari*, Chapter III, part I, Poona: Deccan College.

———, (tr.), 1974, *The Vākyapadīya of Bhartṛhari*, Chapter III, part II, with exegetical notes, Delhi: Motilal Banarsidass.

———, (tr. and ed.), 1975, "Some Lost Works on Vyākaraṇa", in *Sanskrit and Indological Studies*, Delhi: Motilal Banarsidass.

———, (tr.), 1977, *The Vākyapadīya of Bhartṛhari*, Kāṇḍa II, with exegetical notes, Delhi: Motilal Banarsidass.

———, (tr.), 1980, "Bhartṛhari on the Sentence", *Adyar Library Bulletin* 44/45: 15-49.

Jackendoff, Ray, 1983, *Semantics and Cogniton*, Cambridge, MA: MIT.

Jespersen, Otto, 1949, *Language, Its Nature, Development and Origin,* London: George Allen and Unwin.

Jha, Dhanurdhara, 2002, *Vākyārthavivecanam*, Delhi: Nag Publishers.

Jha, Ganganatha, 1942, *Pūrvamīmāṁsā in Its Sources*, Benares: Banaras Hindu University.

Jhalakikar, M. Bhimacharya (ed.), 1978, *Nyāyakośa*, revised and re-edited by V. Shastri Abhyankar, Poona: Bhandarkar Oriental Research Institute.

Jyothirmayi, P.C., 2009, "Indian Theories of Meaning with Special Stress on Bhartṛhari and Chomsky", PhD dissertation, Bangalore University.

Kaviraj, Gopinath M., 1924, "The Doctrine of Pratibhā in Indian Philosophy", *Annals of Bhandarkar Oriental Research Institute,* 5: 113-32.

———, 1963, *The Aspects of Indian Thought*, Calcutta University of Burdwan.

Kieth, A.B., 1928, *A History of Sanskrit Literature*, Oxford: Oxford University Press.

Lakoff, George, 1977, "Linguistic Gestalts", *Proceedings of the Thirteenth Regional Meeting of Chicago Linguistic Society*, ed. W.A. Beach, S.E. Fox and S. Philosoph, pp. 236-87, Chicago: Chicago Linguistic Society.

Langacker, Ronald W., 1987, *Foundations of Cognitive Grammar*, Stanford: Stanford University Press.

Matilal, Bimal Krishna, 1992, *The Word and the World, India's Contribution to the Study of Language*, Delhi: Oxford University Press.

Mazumdar, Pradip Kumar, 1977, *The Philosophy of Language*, Calcutta: Sanskrit Pustak Bhandar.

Mullatti, L.C., 1972, "The Navya-Nyāya Theory of Inference", PhD dissertation, The University of British Columbia.

Murti, M.S. Narayana, 1997, *Bhartṛhari: The Grammarian*, Delhi: Sahitya Akademi.

Patnaik, Tandra, 1989, "Some Reflections on Bhartṛhari's Notion on Sentence Meaning", *The Visva Bharati Journal of Philosophy*, vol. XXIV (2) vol. XXV (1) Feb.-August, 1988, Published in 1989.

———, 1994, *Śabda: A Study of Bhartṛhari's Philosophy of Language*, New Delhi: D.K. Printworld.

Pillai, K. Raghavan (ed. and tr.), 1971, *The Vākyapadīya, Cantos I and II (with English Translation, Summary of Ideas and Notes)*, Delhi: Motilal Banarsidass.

Prasad J., 2010, *The Concept of Pratibhā in Sanskrit Literature*, Calicut: University of Calicut.

Prasad, K.S., 2002, *The Philosophy of Language in Classical Indian Tradition*, New Delhi: Decent Books.

Purushottama, Bilimoria, 2008, *Śabdapramāṇa: Word and Knowledge as Testimony in Indian Philosophy*, New Delhi: D.K. Printworld.

Raja, K. Kunjunni, 1962, "Bhartṛhari's List of Sentence Definitions", *Adyar Library Bulletin,* 26: 206-10.

———, 1963, *Indian Theories of Meaning*, Madras: The Adyar Library and Research Centre.

———, 1994, "Mīmāṁsā Views on Sentence-Meaning: Some Problems", in *Studies in Mīmāṁsā*, ed. R.C. Dwivedi, Delhi: Motilal Banarsidass.

Rao, Veluri Subba, 1969, *The Philosophy of a Sentence and Its Parts*, New Delhi: Munshiram Manoharlal.

Rath, Gayatri, 2000, *Linguistic Philosophy in Vākyapadīya*, Delhi: Bharatiya Vidya Prakashan.

Sarma, K.V., 1969, "Introduction" in *Puruṣārthopadeśa* by Bhartṛhari, ed. K.V. Sarma, Hoshiarpur: Vishveshvaranand Institute.

Sastri, Gaurinath, 1959, *The Philosophy of Word and Meaning*, Calcutta: Sanskrit College.

———, 1980, *A Study in the Dialectics of Sphoṭa*, Delhi: Motilal Banarsidass.

———, 1991, *The Philosophy of Bhartṛhari*, Delhi: Bharatiya Vidya Prakashan.

Sharma, Peri Sarveswara (ed. and tr.), 1972, *The Kālasamuddeśa of Bhartṛhari's Vākyapadīya with the Comm. of Helārāja*, Delhi: Motilal Banarsidass.

———, 1999, *Recent Research in Pāṇinian Studies*, Delhi: Motilal Banarsidass.

Sharma, Punita, 1998, *Concept of Sentence Analysis in Nyāya Philosophy*, Delhi: Nag Publishers.

Smith, Neil, 2004, *Chomsky: Ideas and Ideals*, Cambridge: Cambridge University Press.

Sudhi, Padma, 1983, *Aesthetic Theories of India,* vols I-III, New Delhi: Intellectual Publishing House.

Talmy, Leonard, 1978, "The Relation of Grammar to Cognition", in *Theoretical Issues in Natural Language Processing*, ed. David L. Waltz, pp 14-24, Philadelphia: Association for Computational Linguistics.

Tāranātha, 1990, Tārānāthas *History of Buddhism in India*, ed. Debiprasad Chattopadhyaya, tr. Alka Chattopadhyaya and Lama Chimpa, Delhi Motilal Banarsidass.

Tatacharya, N.S. Ramanuja, 2005, *Śābdabodhamīmāṁsā: An Inquiry into Indian Theories of Verbal Cognition* (part I), New Delhi: Rashtriya Sanskrit Sansthan.

MALAYALAM WORKS

Anandan, K.N., 2003, *Bhāṣā Śāstrattile Chomskyan Viplavam*, Thiruvananthapuram: The State Institute of Languages.

Nair, V.R. Prabodhachandran, 2009, *Bhāṣāśāstradr̥ṣṭiyilūḍe*, Thiruvananthapuram: The State Institute of Languages.

Nampoothiri, E.V.N., 1989, *Vākyaghaṭana*, Thiruvananthapuram: The State Institute of Languages.

Unithiri, N.V.P., 2009, *Śabdārtha Siddhāntaṅgaḷ Saṁskr̥tathil*, Thiruvananthapuram: The State Institute of Languages.

HINDI WORK

Mīmāṁsaka, Yudhiṣṭhira, 1973, *Saṁskr̥ta Vyākaraṇa-śāstra kā Itihāsa* (tīn bhāgoṁ meṁ pūrṇa), Sonepat: Ram Lal Kapur Trust.

Index